**If you've ever been broke,
you'll want to read this book.**

**If you've never been broke,
you need to read this book.**

"While media and popular discourse often spotlight extreme poverty . . . the more heavily cloaked manifestation of poverty in America is the working poor: the millions upon millions who hold down full-time or multiple part-time jobs, often doing hard, dirty, or demeaning minimum-wage tasks, and who can never, it seems, no matter how hard they try, get ahead . . . [Tirado] skewers an entire catalog of myths and misconceptions about the poor, often with fiercely precise humor . . . Welcome and important reporting."
—*The Cleveland Plain Dealer*

"[An] angry, whip-smart woman's firsthand account of what it looks and smells and tastes and feels like to be living in poverty." —*Entertainment Weekly*

"Tirado's raw reportage offers solidarity for those on the front lines of hardship." —*Kirkus Reviews*

"Tirado has a way with words that's somehow both breezy and blunt." —*Bloomberg Businessweek*

continued . . .

HAND
to
MOUTH

LIVING IN BOOTSTRAP AMERICA

Linda Tirado

BERKLEY BOOKS
New York

THE BERKLEY PUBLISHING GROUP
Published by the Penguin Group
Penguin Group (USA) LLC
375 Hudson Street, New York, New York 10014

USA • Canada • UK • Ireland • Australia • New Zealand • India • South Africa • China

penguin.com

A Penguin Random House Company

Berkley trade paperback ISBN: 978-0-425-27797-3

PUBLISHING HISTORY
G. P. Putnam's Sons hardcover edition / October 2014
Berkley trade paperback edition / September 2015

PRINTED IN THE UNITED STATES OF AMERICA

10 9 8 7 6 5 4 3 2 1

Cover design by Nellys Liang.
Interior text design by Meighan Cavanaugh.

While the author has made every effort to provide accurate telephone numbers and Internet
addresses at the time of publication, neither the author nor the publisher is responsible for errors,
or for changes that occur after publication. Further, the publisher does not have any control over
and does not assume any responsibility for author or third-party websites or their content.

*Penguin is committed to publishing works of quality and integrity.
In that spirit, we are proud to offer this book to our readers;
however, the story, the experiences, and the words
are the author's alone.*

For Tom, who can't say I didn't warn him

Contents

Foreword

By Barbara Ehrenreich

I've been waiting for this book for a long time. Well, not this book, because I never imagined that the book I was waiting for would be so devastatingly smart and funny, so consistently entertaining and unflinchingly on target. In fact, I would like to have written it myself—if, that is, I had lived Linda Tirado's life and extracted all the hard lessons she has learned. I am the author of *Nickel and Dimed*, which tells the story of my own brief attempt, as a semi-undercover journalist, to survive on low-wage retail and service jobs. Tirado is the real thing.

After my book came out in 2001, I spent over ten years on the road talking about it at union conferences, church gatherings, and mostly on college campuses. I did this partly for the money because I had lost my best-paying journalistic job in 1997, and then a few years later the media decided that writers no longer needed to be paid at all, as if writing involves no caloric expenditure whatsoever.

But I also did it because I was on a mission. People often asked how my work for *Nickel and Dimed* changed me, and I think they meant how did it make me, as a middle-class person, more aware of the poor. Well, I didn't need that much more awareness since I was born into the lower rung of the working class and managed to re-land in it by becoming a single mother and then marrying a warehouse worker when I was in my thirties. So my stint as a low-wage worker/journalist had only one major effect on me: It moved me from concern about the exploitation of low-wage workers—to something more like rage.

I had expected to experience material deprivation in my life at $7 an hour (the equivalent of about $9 today), and I certainly did. The fact that I had some built-in privileges like a working car (I got a Rent-A-Wreck in each of the cities where I worked so I wouldn't end up writing a book about waiting for buses) only made the deprivation part more shocking. Here I was—in good health, with no small children in my care—working full-time, sometimes more than one job at time, sometimes to the point where my legs felt like rubber, and I was living in a dump and dining at convenience stores or Wendy's.

What I had not expected was the daily humiliation, the insults and what seemed like mean-spirited tricks. To be poor is to be treated like a criminal, under constant suspicion of drug use and theft. It means having no privacy, since the boss has the legal right to search your belongings for stolen items. It involves being jerked around unaccountably, like the time Wal-Mart suddenly changed my schedule, obliterating the second job I had lined up. It means being ordered to "work through" injuries and illness, like the debilitating rash I once acquired from industrial-strength cleaning fluids.

And what was most amazing to me: Being a low-wage worker means being robbed by the very employer who is monitoring *you* so insistently for theft. You can be forced to work overtime without pay or made to start working forty-five minutes before the time clock starts ticking. If you do the math, you may find that a few more hours have been shaved off your paycheck each week by the corporation's computers.

But when I made my way from campus to campus, telling my stories about work and urging students to take an interest in all the low-wage workers who were making their education possible every day—the food service workers, janitors, clerical workers, and adjunct faculty—I was invariably asked the question that boils down to: What's wrong with these people? Meaning the workers, not their bosses.

Typically, the questioner would be a frat boy who had taken Econ 101, a course which exists, as far as I can see, for the sole purpose of convincing young people that the existing class structure is just, fair, and unchangeable anyway. If there's nothing wrong with our economic arrangements, then the only remaining question is: Why do "these people" have children, lack savings, fail to go to college, eat junk food, smoke cigarettes, or whatever else is imagined to be holding them back?

So when I came across Linda Tirado's blog about six months ago, I felt an enormous wave of vindication. Even— or, perhaps, especially—her admission that she smokes cigarettes hit me like a gust of fresh air. She tells what it's like to be a low-wage worker for the long term, with an erratically employed husband and two small children to raise and support. She makes all the points I have been trying to make in my years of campaigning for higher wages and workers' rights: That poverty is not a "culture" or a character defect; it is a shortage of money. And that that shortage arises from grievously inadequate pay, aggravated by constant humiliation and stress, as well as outright predation by employers, credit companies, and even law enforcement agencies.

But let me get out of the way now. She can tell this so much better than I can.

Introduction: Hand to Mouth

In the fall of 2013, I was in my first semester of school in a decade. I had two jobs; my husband, Tom, was working full-time; and we were raising our two small girls. It was the first time in years that we felt like maybe things were looking like they'd be okay for a while.

After a particularly grueling shift at work, I was unwinding online when I saw a question from someone on a forum I frequented: *Why do poor people do things that seem so self-destructive?* I thought I could at least explain what I'd seen and how I'd reacted to the pressures of being poor. I wrote my answer to the question, hit post, and didn't think more about it for at least a few days. This is what it said:

WHY I MAKE TERRIBLE DECISIONS, OR, POVERTY THOUGHTS

There's no way to structure this coherently. They are random observations that might help explain the mental processes. But often, I think that we look at the academic problems of poverty and have no idea of the why. We know the what and the how, and we can see systemic problems, but it's rare to have a poor person actually explain it on their own behalf. So this is me doing that, sort of.

Rest is a luxury for the rich. I get up at 6 a.m., go to school (I have a full course load, but I only have to go to two in-person classes), then work, then I get the kids, then I pick up my husband, then I have half an hour to change and go to Job 2. I get home from that at around 12:30 a.m., then I have the rest of my classes and work to tend to. I'm in bed by 3. This isn't every day, I have two days off a week from each of my obligations. I use that time to clean the house and soothe Mr. Martini and see the kids for longer than an hour and catch up on schoolwork. Those nights I'm in bed by midnight, but if I go to bed too early I won't be able to stay up the other nights because I'll fuck my pattern up, and I drive an hour home from Job 2 so I can't afford to be sleepy. I never get a day off from work unless I am fairly sick. It doesn't leave you much room to think about what you are doing, only to attend to the next thing and the next. Planning isn't in the mix.

When I was pregnant the first time, I was living in a weekly motel for some time. I had a minifridge with no freezer and a microwave. I was on WIC. I ate peanut butter from the jar and frozen burritos because they were 12/$2. Had I had a stove, I couldn't have made beef burritos that cheaply. And I needed the meat, I was pregnant. I might not have had any prenatal care, but I am intelligent enough to eat protein and iron whilst knocked up.

I know how to cook. I had to take Home Ec to graduate high school. Most people on my level didn't. Broccoli is intimidating. You have to have a working stove, and pots, and spices, and you'll have to do the dishes no matter how tired you are or they'll attract bugs. It is a huge new skill for a lot of people. That's not great, but it's true. And if you fuck it up, you could make your family sick. We have learned not to try too hard to be middle class. It never works out well and always makes you feel worse for having tried and failed yet again. Better not to try. It makes more sense to get food that you know will be palatable and cheap and that keeps well. Junk food is a pleasure that we are allowed to have; why would we give that up? We have very few of them.

The closest Planned Parenthood to me is three hours. That's a lot of money in gas. Lots of women can't afford that, and even if you live near one you probably don't want to be seen coming in and out in a lot of areas. We're aware that we are not "having kids," we're "breeding." We have kids for much the same reasons that I imagine rich people do. Urge to propagate and all. Nobody likes poor people procreating, but they judge abortion even harder.

Convenience food is just that. And we are not allowed many conveniences. Especially since the Patriot Act passed, it's hard to get a bank account. But without one, you spend a lot of time figuring out where to cash a check and get money orders to pay bills. Most motels now have a no-credit-card-no-room policy. I wandered around SF for five hours in the rain once with nearly a thousand dollars on me and could not rent a room even if I gave them a $500 cash deposit and surrendered my cell phone to the desk to hold as surety.

Nobody gives enough thought to depression. You have to understand that we know that we will never not feel tired. We will never feel hopeful. We will never get a vacation. Ever. We know that the very act of being poor guarantees that we will never not be poor. It doesn't give us much reason to improve ourselves. We don't apply for jobs because we know we can't afford to look nice enough to hold them. I would make a super legal secretary, but I've been turned down more than once because I "don't fit the image of the firm," which is a nice way of saying "gtfo, pov." I am good enough to cook the food, hidden away in the kitchen, but my boss won't make me a server because I don't "fit the corporate image." I am not beautiful. I have missing teeth and skin that looks like it will when you live on B12 and coffee and nicotine and no sleep. Beauty is a thing you get when you can afford it, and that's how you get the job that you need in order to be beautiful. There isn't much point trying.

Cooking attracts roaches. Nobody realizes that. I've spent a lot of hours impaling roach bodies and leaving them out on toothpick spikes to discourage others from entering. It doesn't work, but is amusing.

"Free" only exists for rich people. It's great that there's a bowl of condoms at my school, but most poor people will never set foot on a college campus. We don't belong there. There's a clinic? Great! There's still a copay. We're not going. Besides, all they'll tell you at the clinic is that you need to see a specialist, which, seriously? Might as well be located on Mars for how accessible it is. "Low-cost" and "sliding scale" sound like "money you have to spend" to me, and they can't actually help you anyway.

I smoke. It's expensive. It's also the best option. You

see, I am always, always exhausted. It's a stimulant. When I am too tired to walk one more step, I can smoke and go for another hour. When I am enraged and beaten down and incapable of accomplishing one more thing, I can smoke and I feel a little better, just for a minute. It is the only relaxation I am allowed. It is not a good decision, but it is the only one that I have access to. It is the only thing I have found that keeps me from collapsing or exploding.

I make a lot of poor financial decisions. None of them matter, in the long term. I will never not be poor, so what does it matter if I don't pay a thing and a half this week instead of just one thing? It's not like the sacrifice will result in improved circumstances; the thing holding me back isn't that I blow five bucks at Wendy's. It's that now that I have proven that I am a Poor Person that is all that I am or ever will be. It is not worth it to me to live a bleak life devoid of small pleasures so that one day I can make a single large purchase. I will never have large pleasures to hold on to. There's a certain pull to live what bits of life you can while there's money in your pocket, because no matter how responsible you are you will be broke in three days anyway. When you never have enough money it ceases to have meaning. I imagine having a lot of it is the same thing.

Poverty is bleak and cuts off your long-term brain.

It's why you see people with four different babydaddies instead of one. You grab a bit of connection wherever you can to survive. You have no idea how strong the pull to feel worthwhile is. It's more basic than food. You go to these people who make you feel lovely for an hour that one time, and that's all you get. You're probably not compatible with them for anything long term, but right this minute they can make you feel powerful and valuable. It does not matter what will happen in a month. Whatever happens in a month is probably going to be just about as indifferent as whatever happened today or last week. None of it matters. We don't plan long term because if we do we'll just get our hearts broken. It's best not to hope. You just take what you can get as you spot it.

I am not asking for sympathy. I am just trying to explain, on a human level, how it is that people make what look from the outside like awful decisions. This is what our lives are like, and here are our defense mechanisms, and here is why we think differently. It's certainly self-defeating, but it's safer. That's all. I hope it helps make sense of it.

While I was thinking that maybe a couple of people would read my essay, lightning struck. A lot of people started to share it. Someone suggested that I submit it for posting on the main page of the website we hung out on. That wasn't uncommon, so I did. The next thing I knew, the world had turned upside down. The Huffington Post ran my essay on its front page, *Forbes* ran it, *The Nation* ran it.

After the original piece went viral, I got a lot of emails from people who told me that they did not agree; they did not cope in the same ways. That's fair, and true. Keep it in mind. What was neither fair nor true was the criticism I received inferring that I was the wrong sort of poor. A lot of this criticism seemed to center on the fact that I was not born into poverty, as though that were the only way someone might find herself unable to make rent. And yet we have a term for it: downward mobility. We have homeless PhDs and more than one recently middle-class person on food stamps. Poverty is a reality to more people than we're willing to admit.

Overall, though, the response was overwhelmingly one of solidarity. I got thousands of emails from people saying that they understood exactly what I was trying to describe, that they felt the same way. They told me their stories—the things that bothered them and how they were dealing with life. It's not just me who feels this way, not by a long shot. Poor people talk about these things, but no one's listening to us. We don't usually get a chance to explain our own logic. The original piece that you just read, and this book, are simply that: explanations. I am doing what I can to walk you through what it is to be poor. To be sure, this is only one version. There are millions of us; our experiences and reactions to them are as varied as our personalities and backgrounds.

I haven't had it worse than anyone else, and actually, that's kind of the point. This is just what life is for roughly a third of the country. We all handle it in our own ways, but we all work in the same jobs, live in the same places, feel the same sense of never quite catching up. We're not any happier about the exploding welfare rolls than anyone else is, believe me. It's not like everyone grows up and dreams of working two essentially meaningless part-time jobs while collecting food stamps. It's just that there aren't many other options for a lot of people.

In fact, the Urban Institute found that half of Americans will experience poverty at some point before they're sixty-five. Most will come out of it after a relatively short time, 75 percent in four years. But that still leaves 25 percent who don't get out quickly, and the study also found that the longer you stay in poverty, the less likely it becomes that you will ever get out.

Most people who live near the bottom go through cycles of being in poverty and being just above it—sometimes they're just okay and sometimes they're underwater. It depends on the year, the job, how healthy you are. What I can say for sure is that downward mobility is like quicksand. Once it grabs you, it keeps constraining your options until it's got you completely.

I slid to the bottom through a mix of my own decisions and some seriously bad luck. I think that's true of most people. While it can seem like upward mobility is blocked by a lead ceiling, the layer between lower-middle class and poor is horrifyingly porous from above. A lot of us live in that spongy divide.

I got here in a pretty average way: I left home at sixteen for college, promptly behaved as well as you'd expect a teenager to, and was estranged from my family for over a decade. I quit college when it became clear that I was taking out loans to no good effect; I wasn't ready for it yet. I chased a career simply because it was the first opportunity available rather than because it was sensible.

And I also had medical bills. I had bouts of unemployment, I had a drunken driver total my car. I had everything I owned destroyed in a flood.

So it's not just one or the other: nature or nurture, poor or not poor. Poverty is a potential outcome for all of us.

This is a huge societal problem, and we're just starting to come to grips with all the ways that a technological revolution and globalization have vastly increased inequality. You cannot blame your average citizen for those things. Nor can you blame individual companies—it is how we, collectively, have decided to do things.

We got here partially because of bad policy decisions and partially because of factors nobody could have foreseen. Telling an individual company to do better is a lot like telling an individual poor person to save more—true and helpful, but not so easy in practice. Most companies, like most people, aren't the top 1 percent. They are following the market, not driving it. Besides which, any asshole with money can buy and run a company. They're not all smart enough to figure out long-term investments in human capital.

I am not, for all my frustration, opposed to capitalism. Most Americans, poor ones included, aren't. We like the idea that anyone can succeed. What I am opposed to is the sort of capitalism that sucks the life out of a whole bunch of the citizenry and then demands that they do better with whatever they have left. If we could just agree that poor people are doing the necessary grunt work and that there is dignity in that too, we'd be able to make it less onerous.

Put another way: I'm not saying that *someone* doesn't have to scrub the toilets around here. All I'm saying is that maybe instead of being grossed out by the very idea of toilets, you could thank the people doing the cleaning, because if not for them, you'd have to do it your damn self.

In this book I have been careful to obscure identifying

details about people. Most of the people I've worked for have long since turned over themselves and work elsewhere now. Just in case, however, I have changed places, personal details, and names as needed to protect people's privacy. Nobody, myself included, thought that I'd be writing a book.

A note about the definitions of certain words used in this book: These are my definitions, but I'll tell you what they are up front. *Poverty* is when a quarter is a fucking miracle. *Poor* is when a dollar is a miracle. *Broke* is when five bucks is a miracle. *Working class* is being broke, but doing so in a place that might not be run-down. *Middle class* is being able to own some toys and to live in a nice place—and by "nice," I don't mean fancy; I mean that you can afford to buy your own furniture and not lease it and that while you still worry about bills, you aren't constantly worried about homelessness. And *rich* is anything above that.

This book is not exhaustive, but it is a collection of some of the emotions and experiences I've had while trying to get back to the starting line. Some of these are illogical. Some are counterintuitive. Some are contradictory. That's because I am a human being, and we are all of those things.

There are also many things that I am not. Instead of attempting to point out how people who are different from me are in many ways far more disadvantaged than I have ever been in every instance I can think of (because that should be clear unless you have the peripheral vision of a race-horse), I will just say this: Here is how I have felt, *as me*: as a relatively young person who is perceived as white, who is naturally sociable, who is intelligent and well-spoken, who was taught well and as a result loves learning things, who is able to lift objects up to fifty pounds repeatedly. And many times, with all of that going for me, I still saw no hope. I cannot begin to imagine how much harder it is for someone who faces more discrimination than I have or who grew up without these basic tools that I am lucky enough to have. Keep that in mind too.

I would lastly like this to be clear: I haven't spent a lot of time talking about the good things in my life—my loves and interests and friends. Those exist, because—again—I'm human. Those things are common to all humans, and for now you're interested in the things that are unique to the poor, and how we cope with them. I've focused on the things I've been most often criticized for in my life and explained the motivations as I see them. I'm here to tell you why *this* person does what she does.

So take a tour with me through some of the aspects of life that poverty impacts and on which poor people are judged: our work ethics (or lack thereof), our sex lives (definitely way too much of that), our coping mechanisms (naughty poor people), our health practices (I know, you still can't believe that I smoke). And so on. Stick with me. It won't always be easy, but maybe you'll learn something about the lives of your fellow Americans in the process.

And truthfully? What I'm really hoping is that you'll learn something about yourself and that maybe you'll start thinking a bit differently.

So now, the book. Thank you for being open-minded. If you've made it this far (I planted some test profanity in here just to make sure we're on the same page), you might understand what I'm on about.

HAND
to
MOUTH

1

It Takes Money to Make Money

When I tried to come up with my worst, most exemplary terrible job to start off this chapter, I found myself a little bit stuck. Let's just say I have an embarrassment of riches to choose from. But here's one:

I was in my mid-twenties, married, childless. My husband and I lived in a small town in the mountains at the time. I was working as a bartender. If you have ever wondered where frat boys go to die, it's to grown-up fraternal organizations. They have their own members-only bars and pretty much feel like they can do whatever they want inside their members-only walls. And that included, at this place, violating the physical and mental boundaries of those of us serving them their drinks.

During NASCAR races, we would have dozens of people sitting around drinking Bud Light and arguing the relative merits of Junior. (For the uninitiated, that's Dale Earnhardt Jr. There is a raging debate about the relative merits of Junior versus his daddy, although both are beloved. If you are in the country and you mention Junior by his given name, you will have immediately outed yourself as city folk.) I had two bosses: One was nearing eighty and mostly just wanted to drink copious amounts of rotgut while pretending to manage the books. The other was in his prime—or at least he'd never lived a day in his life in which he didn't think he looked amazing. (Really, he was balding and portly and had a molester mustache. Let's call him M.M. for short.)

M.M. liked to remark on how young I was and then "accidentally" brush against the parts of me that didn't usually see daylight. He wasn't there every day, but when he was, I could look forward to being asked every twenty minutes or so whether I'd be willing to service him sexually. The fact that his wife was often within earshot mattered not at all, because *of course* he was only joshing, proving how virile he still was. Except that the women who did sleep with him got the better shifts. Funny, right?

I wasn't desperate enough to do that for an extra $20 or $30 a day. (There is definitely an amount of money you could pay me to have sex with a skeevy old dude, but I'm fairly certain I've priced myself well out of M.M.'s financial reach.) Instead, I'd make my minimum wage and maybe another $10 or $20 in tips, leaving me with a grand total of enough income to qualify me for state aid.

So I picked up a second job waiting tables. The thing about working for tips is that you're supposed to always make at least the minimum wage. The federal minimum for waiting tables is $2.13 an hour (some states do have higher minimums for tipped employees, but only about half of them). If you don't make enough in tips to bump you up to the federal minimum wage of $7.25, the restaurant is supposed to kick in the difference. Corporate restaurants are too protective of their bottom lines to allow a single useless employee, so they typically send waitstaff home as soon as they can. The smaller mom-and-pop places, where there might be only a single waitperson on staff for hours at a time when it's slow, might have their employees do deep cleaning and other things when there are no customers. So there you are, working constantly but getting paid only $2.13 an hour. No matter how good a waitress you are, you probably won't make two or three hours' worth of minimum wage out of tips from your only table in hours. These aren't the kind of restaurants where generous patrons just take it into their heads to overtip. And if you remind your boss that he is supposed to top you off to $7.25, then you run the risk of finding yourself with reduced hours or fired altogether. So you pretty much keep your mouth shut about that.

My second job: I made $4 an hour or so at that one, because new people get the slow shifts. Hours would go by in which not a single customer walked in. Let me run you through the math on this one: On an average day, I'd work for six or seven hours. I might make $50. Some days were better, some worse. I couldn't take the busy dinner shifts at the restaurant even after I was trained, because I was at my first job until the middle of dinner rush and the restaurant needed its dinner staff in the door by midafternoon to prep. Meanwhile, I missed special events like picnics and the like at the bar that I might have made money on because I was at the restaurant.

And this is how it goes. Every time I've had more than one job, I've missed out on as much cash as I've made because of scheduling issues. Getting a second job wouldn't be worth it at all except for the fact that those special events and extra hours are never guaranteed in advance. If it's a week with no extra shifts, or with bad weather that keeps customers home, you're stuck. So you hedge that bet by finding another shitty job.

The most I've seen anyone manage at once was four jobs: bartending, dancing, waitressing, and teaching yoga. I've held down up to three: tending bar, waiting tables, and working as a voter registration canvasser. It nearly killed me, and I still didn't break twenty grand that year.

I think that most liberal Americans don't have too hard a

time believing that it's difficult to make ends meet when you're making minimum wage. But I also think that people in both parties get hung up on the minimum wage as some kind of miracle line of demarcation—as if making more than the minimum puts you on easy street. Meanwhile, millions of people are making above minimum wage—so they don't get counted as making the minimum. And do you know what they're making? Instead of $7.25 an hour, they're getting $7.35 an hour. Maybe even $7.50! In many places in America—think fast-food restaurants, dollar stores, gas stations—most of the employees make under $8 or $9. And these employees are not all kids. So when you hear or participate in these discussions about minimum wage statistics, assume that the vast majority of service workers are making within a stone's throw of minimum wage. Our ladder's rungs are set close together, and there are so many of them that it takes us forever to climb it. My husband worked for the same restaurant for nearly two years before he broke $7.75. Was he making minimum? No. But the difference between minimum wage and $7.75 is just around $1,040 a year if you're working full-time, which is pretty rare.

So there you are, working all the time, bringing home so little, and very often getting behind. But your landlord doesn't care that you're working as hard as you can, that there aren't more hours for you to work. The only thing that matters to your landlord is whether or not you have the money for the rent. I've had a landlord tell me that I could be turning tricks if I really cared about paying my bills, that clearly the only reason I was broke is that I wasn't trying hard enough, that he had no patience for people who couldn't simply get along in life. He actually dispensed all of this as though it were helpful advice rather than a series of insults. And that was *after* the begging, after I'd already debased myself, already explained that my hours got cut for the slow season and they hadn't warned me in time for me to find another job.

This is my bottom-line point about work and poverty: It's far more demoralizing to work and be poor than to be unemployed and poor. I have never minded going without when I wasn't working. It sucks not to be able to find a job, but you expect to be tired and pissed off and to never be able to leave your house when you're flat broke. Working your balls off, begging for more hours, hustling every penny you can, and still not being able to cover your electric bill with any regularity is soul-killing.

The popular conception of minimum wage workers is that they're mostly teenagers working part-time. That would be because the Bureau of Labor Statistics, on its website, is pretty clear that about half of workers making the minimum or below are under the age of twenty-five. But that same BLS website will tell you that about half of workers making the minimum or below are *not* under the age of twenty-five. That's 800,000 adults over the age of twenty-five working at minimum wage or below. Or, if you prefer, about 25,000 more people than live in all of San Francisco.

As I've pointed out already, a lot of adults are getting just pennies over the minimum wage—and I'd argue that your average adult does his job, however lowly, a damn sight better than most teenagers. And when you think about how insignificant a raise of even fifty cents above the minimum turns out to be, it's hard not to feel devalued—as if the sum of your accomplishments as an adult amounts to some nickels and dimes.

But let's put that frustration aside and talk about what it actually means to make minimum wage.

Working for minimum wage (or, as we've already established, close to it) means that making a long-term budget is an exercise in wishful thinking. You just have however much money you have until you run out, and you pay whatever bill is most overdue first. When I was working in Ohio at a fast-food joint, I'd generally get about twenty-five hours in a week. That was paid at $7.50, making my weekly check $187.50. My husband, working forty hours at the same place, brought home $300. We made about $25,000 or so between us, working every week of the year. That's a little over $9,000 above the poverty line for a family of two, or an extra $200 or so a week. We made ends meet, but barely. Not well enough to ever really feel comfortable or rest or take a day off without feeling guilty. And we were at the top of the bottom third of households that year, meaning that approximately one-third of the America population is living on the same sort of budget.

Or, for some, a much smaller one. The yearly income of a forty-hour-a-week minimum-wage worker is $15,080. So if you're paying half of that for housing, you're left with $7,540 to live on.

Yearly.

That's $628 per month, or $314 per paycheck, for everything else—food, clothes, car payments, gas. If you're lucky, you get all that money to live on. But who's lucky all of the time, or even most of the time? Maybe you get sick and lose your job. Even if you land a new job, that measly $314 is all you've got to last you until your paychecks at the new place start up. Or what if, God forbid, the car breaks down or you break a bone?

But all right, let's increase that salary. Let's be kind and bump it up well above the median fast-food worker's pay. If you're doing okay, making, say, $10 an hour, that's $20,800. That leaves you $10,400 to live on annually, $867 monthly, $433 per paycheck. Before taxes. (Which, by the way, we pay plenty of.) Not that $100 doesn't make a giant difference, but it's not like you're rolling around in money like

Scrooge McDuck simply because you're earning better than the absolute least that can be legally paid.

Of course, those scenarios are if you are absolutely jacked, with half of your income going to rent. If we go with the old one-third recommendation, then your disposable income by paycheck rises a bit, to $418 for those making minimum and $577 if you're at double digits.

So, let's go with the more generous number. Say you make $10 an hour and you pay a third of that in rent. That's going to give you $1,066 a month to spend. You pay your utilities and for gas to get to work. Food and household stuff. Maybe you now have $500 left. And that's assuming, of course, that you have no medical bills or prescriptions or debts. And that's before taxes.

The truth is that what you've got left from all that work you've been doing is about $10 per day to spend on anything other than the barest necessities—and that's based on the premise that you live in a shitty apartment, eat cheaply, and work full-time with no missed days. Then, if you do all of those things and you are unburdened by debt and medical issues, you can do any number of things with your free time! You can rent a movie and buy microwave popcorn. You can drive to the nicer section of town and have fancy coffee. With $10 a day to spend at whim, the world is your oyster. Hell, you could even buy a can of oysters.

I'm hoping that I'm not being too subtle here, because

this is what it comes down to: The math doesn't fucking work. You can't thrive on this sort of money. Period. You can survive. That's it.

There is something even worse than minimum wage. It's called temp work. I bet that the majority of Americans— unless they've experienced it for themselves—would be shocked to find out that companies regularly hire temps to work full-time hours, but because they hire these workers through temporary work agencies, they have to pay no benefits and offer no job security. To save a buck, companies will regularly hire such workers for years—*years*. And they do it because it's cheaper than hiring labor directly, and they are legally entitled to do so. The laws in this country are so weak that we're actually way behind South Korea (!) in temp worker protections.

So when financially comfortable people with health insurance and paid sick leave and all kinds of other benefits that pad their wallets and make their lives easier and healthier think that the poor are poor because somehow we lack the get-up-and-go to change our circumstances . . . well, I'm not sure my reaction is printable.

I regularly thank the gods that I don't have much experience working in the temp industry. I've got friends that do, though, and it's pretty awful. You get to work for a company full-time, as anything from a janitor to an attorney, but you don't get any benefits and they sure as hell aren't telling you to count on keeping this paycheck. They don't guarantee anything. You might have worked there for years, but as long as they keep hiring you through the agency, they can save on pesky things like raises and promotions. One plant I lived near used to hire a revolving number of temp workers whom they laid off after ninety days—the point at which a temp worker is supposed to get permanent job status. Then after three weeks of unemployment, the plant hired them again.

That factory isn't in town anymore. It had gotten a break from the local government, making its first years there tax-free. And wouldn't you know it, after the tax break expired, the company decided that the plant wasn't profitable enough and closed it. A temporary factory that hired temporary workers.

Who says capitalism isn't cruel?

2

You Get What You Pay For

As far as I'm concerned, I earn my wages with my scars. Anything above and beyond that is me doing my employers a favor. And I'm not inclined to do favors for people who treat me poorly. See, we work in insane conditions. Dangerous, even. Most kitchens in the middle of the summer are intolerable, with temperatures well into the triple digits. I've seen people sent to the hospital with heatstroke. A lot of us will run into the freezer for a few minutes until we cool down. I'm not a doctor and I can't say for sure, but I'm fairly certain that going from overheated to a minus-5 environment can't be healthy.

My arms and hands are covered in scars from the fryers. Oil at nearly 400 degrees doesn't tickle when it hits your skin, and you can't avoid the spatter entirely. I've burned my hands because the oven gloves had worn through and the owners were too cheap to spring for another pair. I've sliced my fingers open nearly to the bone when knives have slipped. I've dropped equipment on my feet because it was so busy I didn't have time to wash the grease off my hands. I've hurt myself in more ways than I can count because that was how I got my seven or eight bucks an hour.

Stuff like that is unavoidable; it's the nature of the work. We know and understand that when we take the jobs. Any dangerous job is like that; we're not stupid. The point is more that the risk is devalued—that our injuries, rather than being seen as a sign of our willingness to literally bleed for our employers, are seen as a liability.

The kitchen scars are more dramatic, but the emotional toll of retail is the worst. The conditions are patently impossible. I've been expected to spend three hours per shift stocking in the back, while also being told that the register was never to be left unattended. I've been told to always have coffee ready for customers and that it should always be fresh, and in the same breath been told that I was going through too much coffee. My section of the store is always supposed to be neat, but there's only one of me and over three hundred square feet to cover, and there are shoppers everywhere and not enough racks for all this shit to begin with.

My shoe size actually changed with the quality of the jobs I've had. The better ones let me sit down sometimes. At the not-so-nice ones, I've stood for eight to ten hours, and my feet have gotten so swollen that my shoes don't fit.

The mandatory cheerleading is why I never worked for Walmart. Apparently this has changed now, but during employee meetings, they used to require their people to actually cheer. With pelvic thrusting. (Go watch the YouTube videos. It must be seen to be believed.) In those not long ago days, if you didn't wiggle your ass with sufficient vigor, you'd find yourself on the wrong side of management and then brought to the front to lead the cheer yourself. Sure, give me a W and an A and an L and a squiggly (or I guess now it's an asterisk since they rebranded), and I will happily shove them straight up your ass. Friends of mine will swear that they never got demerits until after they upset management by lacking enthusiasm. (To be fair to Wal*Mart, my friends weren't actually let go because they wouldn't wiggle enough. They can't prove causation. It's just that they didn't start getting demerits until they stopped wiggling.)

At work, I'm often told what words to say, and I will be written up if I deviate from the script or combine two steps to save time. In retail, we must acknowledge a customer who comes within a set radius of us with a certain tone and tenor in our voices. In telemarketing, our every word might be scripted. In fast food, we're typically given three greetings

LINDA TIRADO

to choose from. At one large fast-food chain (let's call it LFC for short), the choices were these:

1) Welcome to LFC, how can I help you?
2) Welcome to LFC, would you like to try a delicious chicken meal today for only $4.99?
3) Welcome to LFC, what can we make fresh for you today?

The company even sent in undercover customers to make sure we stayed on script.

All of our actions are carefully dictated to us. I assume this is because employers think we have monkey brains and are incapable of making decisions. This means that they're paying me to pretend I'm not me and also that I care about you.

And as long as we're on the topic of insane things your bosses can do, you should be aware that you have no legal right to take breaks in America. Go ahead, Google it. Some states mandate breaks. Some farmwork has a federal break mandate. But overall, you've no right to demand a lunch break or a break at all. That's all at the discretion of your employer.

Some people have the luxury of asking themselves whether a job fulfills their career hopes and ambitions. I've got my own metric to gauge the fabulosity of a job: Does that

job require me to keep my boss informed of the inner work-
ings of my gastrointestinal system, or am I allowed to go to
the bathroom at will? It's physically uncomfortable to hold it
forever, and it sucks to stand by for the okay like a dog waiting for someone to open the door. But for me, the indignity
of the whole thing is less about the potential bladder infec-
tions. It's more what the requirement for that kind of notifi-
cation reveals about the tone of the place. In my experience,
the jobs where the boss regulates your urinary tract also
tend to demand a bunch of other degrading stuff.

We all know that a lot of folks think that poor people are
lazy and incompetent. They think we get fired from jobs
because we don't know how to behave, or we're always late,
or we just don't care. But what rich people don't realize is
how unbelievably easy it is to get fired. And a lot of times
what gets you fired is that you're working more than one job.

Whenever you are working for the kind of place that has
a corporate office, you're typically given the fewest possible
hours—definitely less than full-time, because then they'd
have to pay you benefits. (Full-time is often in the twenty-
eight- to thirty-two-hours-a-week range, to boot.) But even
though your employer might schedule you for twenty hours
a week, you might wind up working ten, or thirty. It depends

on how busy it is—when it's slow, they send you home, and when it's busy, they expect you to stay late. They also expect you to be able to come in to cover someone's shift if a co-worker gets sick at the last minute. Basically, they're expecting you to be available to work all the time. Scheduling is impossible.

At one chain, I was required to sign a contract stating that I was an at-will employee, that I would be part-time with no benefits, and that if I took another job without permission, I would be subject to termination because the company expected me to be able to come in whenever they found it necessary. And yes, this is legal in the United States of America.

It's unavoidable; even I have had to admit the impossibility of this system and let people go, one an employee that I actually liked very much. Competent, friendly, good sense of humor. But her other boss simply would not post the schedule far enough in advance for me to give the woman any hours. If the workweek started Monday, the schedule at her other job went up Sunday night. I tried to do my scheduling a week or more in advance, and when I called the other restaurant to discuss the issue, the manager told me that she didn't actually feel any need to change her routines and that it was my problem to deal with. I simply had to let the woman go, because her other boss wanted the availability.

How is that legal, you ask? Well, a huge number of jobs

in this country—and a crazy high percentage of the jobs that poor people hold down—are considered at-will. Sometimes you'll sign a paper stating that you understand what that means, sometimes not. It depends on the sophistication and size of the business hiring you. What "at-will" means is that your boss can decide that your eyes are too brown one day and let you go on the spot. As long as they're not in violation of civil rights law, they don't have to give you a reason, and they can decide that anything is a fireable offense. I've been fired because my boss made a mistake on some paperwork. I've been fired because I had the flu. I've been fired because I wouldn't sleep with someone. I've been fired because I *did* sleep with someone. I once saw a stripper fired because she couldn't afford breast implants and the club manager didn't find her natural breasts alluring enough to dance topless for drunken construction workers.

So let's break this down: You're poor, so you desperately need whatever crappy job you can find, and the nature of that crappy job is that you can be fired at any time. Meanwhile, your hours can be cut with no notice, and there's no obligation on the part of your employer to provide severance regardless of why, how, or when they let you go. And we wonder why the poor get poorer?

Of course not every firing is part of an intricate plot by the plutocrats. I've also been fired for calling off work too much ("calling off work," for those unfamiliar with the vernacular, just means that you call your boss to say you're not coming in). Usually I've called off because I was legitimately sick, because I rarely miss work more than I can help. But sometimes it was because my car wouldn't start or because I just couldn't face it. It doesn't matter what you say, and your boss doesn't care; the point is whether you do it too much, not whether your reasons are legit.

I admit it—I've been fired for doing some stupid shit. I've been fired for consistent tardiness because I simply didn't care, and more than once because I gave my boss the finger. And as a manager, I've fired people for being dumbasses—stuff like showing up to work too hung over to stand up straight. Once I had to fire a guy because he went and got knuckle tattoos. I've even fired someone for relentless creepiness. That was the one time I thanked God for at-will states. He wasn't a terrible worker, and there was nothing to point to, but he did brush his groin with his hand once too often while looking at the girls up front.

Idiot pranks are risky too. One kid I worked with got bored and built a castle out of cardboard boxes in the parking lot. They fired him a) because it made the company "look unprofessional," and b) for "time theft." I've seen someone get fired, no shit, because he didn't want to wear buttons proclaiming him proficient at cleaning and other menial tasks. I barely made it through the day without mentioning

TPS reports. (If you don't know what those are, drop everything and go watch *Office Space* right now.)

Mostly, I've fired people because they didn't care about
the things that do matter to me. I've never cared any more for
the owners of the companies I've worked for than they have
for me, but I will kill myself for my co-workers. A lot of us do
that. When we work through fevers and injuries and bone
weariness, it's for the money but also because if we don't, we
know that we'll be leaving our co-workers holding the bag.
However bad the shift is, with a man down, it'll be that much
worse on whoever's left. There's a siege mentality in the service industry in particular; you go through hell together. If
you tap out and go home, you're leaving your co-workers to
deal with more customers with even fewer hands. And that
means that they're more likely to get fired themselves—
because if customers start complaining about the service,
the boss doesn't really care that you're covering for someone
who's out sick. So you bet your sweet ass that if you work for
me and I see you being dead weight, I'll get rid of you.

All of this is not to cast myself as some kind of paragon
of work perfection. I'm a terrible corporate manager, every
time I tried it. My employees loved me, but I made a lousy
guardian of profit margins. My first loyalty is to my co-
workers. Then the customers. And then, in a distant third,
the company.

For example, when I found out that some of my employees had themselves a fantastic gig pulling the expired salad and bruised or unusable produce out of the Dumpster and taking it home, I started making sure that the food was disposed of *next to* the trash rather than in it. This, you should know, was highly against the rules on everyone's part.

I figured if I got busted, I'd just say that I was trying to keep track of how much got thrown away to help me order properly the next time. I'm not sure what the company would have done if they'd found out; most companies simply don't want to know about stuff like that because even they don't want to be that harsh, but liability exists. No restaurant can knowingly allow anyone to eat expired food, even if it's obviously still sound. With that said, companies also discourage letting employees eat unservable food because they assume that a worker would have bought food instead of just going without, and heaven knows it's a sin to lose potential profits from workers! Only, most people don't buy their food half-off at their own stores; most people just drink more on hungry shifts when they can't eat. I always figured that my cooks would probably not be doing their best work if they were salivating every time some food finished cooking. And I just couldn't live with myself letting these guys look longingly at the burgers they were flipping as if they were Victorian street urchins lusting after a hot roll in a bakery window.

If one of my people was hungry, I gave them food. I'd

send parents home with boxes of expired chicken nuggets for their kids. My bosses, of course, generally hated dealing with me. It's been a pattern. I don't really blame them—their jobs sucked as much as mine did and I was a huge pain in their asses. One of my favorite bosses once told me that he hated having to explain the *why* of everything to me, but I considered it my job to be able to explain the why to the people who reported to me. If hours were getting cut or pay frozen, I damn well was going to give them a reason that made sense. If we were going to lay off a quarter of the staff, I'd better be able to explain it.

I know a lot of people think that I'm supposed to be a good little worker bee and do my part to help move the wheels of capitalism. I just don't see what's in it for me anymore beyond my little paycheck. Think about it this way: At my earning peak, I made approximately nineteen cents a minute before taxes.

So when I go out of my way to work hard, I'm not doing it for my bosses, I'm doing it for my co-workers. There's definitely a mutual covering of asses going on in the lower classes. (Hey, why should the upper classes do all the ass covering?) I've even tracked down babysitters for employees who'd lost their child care and couldn't afford to lose their shift as well. Instead of letting an employee call off work and winding up shorthanded to boot, I called around until I found a cashier who was more than happy to babysit for a few hours for some extra cash. I loaned the cook the money to pay the cashier, and everyone got something they needed. We do shit like that a lot.

We'd never survive otherwise.

Once I'm home from my shift, I try not to be short-tempered with my husband, whose fault my bad mood decidedly isn't. In turn, he tries not to be short-tempered with me. Working at a low-wage job means getting off work and having just enough mental energy to realize what you could be doing with your life . . . if only you could work up the will to physically move.

And honestly, I wouldn't even mind the degradations of my work life so much if the privileged and powerful were honest about it. If they just admitted that this is simply impossible. Instead, we're told to work harder and be grateful we have jobs, food, and a roof over our heads. And for fuck's sake, we are. But in exchange for all that work we're doing, and all our miserable work conditions, we're not allowed to demand anything in return. No sense of accomplishment, or respect from above, or job security. We are expected not to feel entitled to these things. Being poor while working hard is fucking crushing. It's living in a nightmare where the walls just never stop closing in on you.

I resent the fuck out of it every time my schedule's been cut and then I've been called in for tons of extra hours, as though my time weren't worth anything, just so that my boss can be sure not to pay me for a minute that I'm not absolutely necessary. I resent signing away my ability to get a second job and being told that I can't work more than twenty-eight hours a week either.

The result of all of this? I just give up *caring* about work. I lose the energy, the bounce, the willingness. I'll perform as directed, but no more than that. I've rarely had a boss who gave me any indication that he valued me more highly than my uniform—we were that interchangeable—so I don't go out of my way for my bosses either. The problem I have isn't just being undervalued—it's that it feels as though people go out of their way to make sure you know how useless you are.

I'd been working for one company for over a year when I injured myself at work in November and had to go on leave for two months because I couldn't stand for long. So I wasn't invited to the company Christmas party. I went as a co-worker's date and watched as everyone got their Christmas bonuses. I didn't get one; I was technically not in the managerial position and thus didn't qualify. The fact that I'd worked the rest of the year didn't count.

What really got me, though, was when the owner of the company thanked the woman who was filling in for me for working so hard all year. He didn't recognize me at all.

With unwavering support like that, it's not really a mystery why I've rarely felt huge personal drive to make more money for the people signing my checks. I'm as loyal as they pay me to be, basically. Most of the people I know are the same way. It's only logical. See, if we perform really well, give it a full 120 percent, we might make shift manager. That's a whole extra $2 an hour. For that $2 or so, we get to be in the direct line of fire for the profit margins. We get to be held responsible for things outside our control.

And we get to be stuck.

If you're working at your typical service job, shift manager is about as high as you can get, because for every four or six shift managers, there's only one general manager position. But let's say that the company treats everyone so poorly that turnover is high. Then you might make assistant or even general manager, at which point you'll earn somewhere between $20,000 and $35,000 in exchange for physically punishing, emotionally draining eighty- or ninety-hour weeks. (Salaries in cities are generally higher, but both companies I worked for capped out in the mid-$30,000 range.) I'll put it this way: As general manager for a chain restaurant, I got eight days of maternity leave after I had my second daughter. Unpaid.

It's not like we don't wish for more, but really, what's the better option? School is an investment that doesn't make sense for people who aren't the academic sort. You have to pay cash money for it, you can't hold down as many hours at work, it's harder to find work because your schedule's inflexible, and dear God the cost of textbooks is enough to kill you. Hell, I *am* the academic sort, and for many years school wasn't a good investment for me. It left me in debt with nothing to show for it.

Before I moved into the service economy, I tried to make a more fulfilling, less backbreaking living working in political organizing. To be clear: The jobs that I worked at in politics weren't exactly highly paid either. They were typically in the $8 to $10 hourly range. I laughed my ass off when people went digging through my financial history after my essay on poverty was published and found the Federal Election Commission filings of my political pay. (Pro tip for amateur PI sorts: Those numbers? That's how much I got for the *whole year*, not per paycheck. Seriously, how much do you really think they pay someone to knock on doors or co-ordinate other people doing it?) The dark truth of many fulfilling, creative jobs and industries is that you are expected to accept very little pay at the start, just for the privilege of learning the ropes and working your way up. And that's fine if you've got Mom and Dad helping you. But if not, you tend not to go into those fields. Which means that the people who do go into those fields are often pretty privileged; not many Congressional staffers come out of the lower class.

And it's not just about how little you are paid in fields like politics. It's also the stuff you're expected to do in addition. For example, there are constant training sessions during the off-season. Most of them cost money and are held in Washington, DC. All of my friends who still work in politics went to them. I didn't. All of my friends who took short-term, low-pay jobs with people who could be mentors are still working in politics. I had to turn those jobs down—the ones I was offered, anyway. Often I didn't even bother to send in my résumé in the first place, because I knew I couldn't afford to work for so little. Mostly, I found myself perpetually stuck on the bottom rung, watching people I'd started out with vault above me because they weren't doing anything but this and they could afford to take the financial hits while they were paying their dues.

Here's another thing the poor can't afford: unpaid internships. I've had to turn down offers that might have improved my circumstances in the long run because I just couldn't afford to work for nothing. Again, the people who can afford unpaid internships are getting help from home—in my world, everyone else has to work for a living. And this means that we're being cut out of all that potential networking too. That's at least one reason why I've never had much of a professional network—I never had the chance to build one. Accepting an unpaid internship, or one of those internships that basically pays you lunch money, is for people who don't have to pay the rent.

Because I've always been in a take-what-you-can-get situation, I've wound up working the sorts of jobs that people consider beneath them. And yet people still wonder why we, working at the bottom, aren't putting our souls into our jobs. In turn, I wonder about people who think that those who are poor shouldn't demand reciprocity from their employers. We should devote ourselves to something that doesn't benefit us more than it absolutely has to? We're meant to care about their best interests, but they don't have to care about ours? If you're going to put as little as possible into my training and wages, if you're going to make sure that I can't get enough hours to survive in order to avoid giving me health care, and generally make sure that I'm as uncomfortable as possible at any given time just to make sure I know my place, then how can you expect me to care about your profit margin?

Remember, you get what you pay for.

3

You Can't Pay a
Doctor in Chickens
Anymore

Excruciating should be defined in the dictionary as an exposed nerve. Once I killed nearly a whole bottle of vodka in the space of a night, and I'm not a frequent drinker. I was at least six shots gone before the pain started to fade into blessed numbness.

It took me a few years of the long slide into poverty to cotton on to the unavailability of anything besides crisis medical care. I'd come from a home in which we went to the doctor when we needed to. Dad had benefits. It never occurred to me as a kid to question it. And it took me a while as an adult to understand that without benefits, which no longer come standard-issue with your average job like they used to, hospital administrators would rather you die on the street than sully their expensive sheets. (And the sheets are expensive. Like the Tylenol. Whole books have been written about that, and I can't do the subject justice in a few paragraphs, but don't think we don't know that they charge us triple for those lifesaving medications because we are not rich enough to have other rich people negotiate better prices for us.)

Being healthy and being poor are generally mutually exclusive conditions. We all have physical weaknesses, but a rich person gets these tended to before they get out of control. Poor people don't have that luxury. So it's pretty enraging to poor people when rich people, who get preventive care and can afford vitamins and gym memberships, look down on us as if we don't have a clue how to take care of our bodies. We know—we just can't afford it.

Dentistry is one of the things we are most lacking in. And it's one of the most glaring marks of poverty. I watch the tooth-bleaching ads and cringe, because I know exactly what I'm being pegged as. Incapable. Uneducated. Oblivious. What I should be pegged as: uninsured, and until recently, uninsurable.

I did get some dental surgery once. I had five teeth pulled and a partial denture built so that at least I would have front teeth. I think I was nearly twenty-six at the time. I made an appointment, which took all the force of will I had. I got in the chair at the office, and promptly listened to forty-five straight minutes of the most upsetting, judgmental lecture I'd ever received in my life. This woman, the dentist, decided that I must be on meth. (I'd like to make this point clear: I have never in my life done meth. Ever. Other drugs, sure, but not this one in particular. It seems to me that because I have failed so much, been weak so often, I am prouder of those things I have managed to avoid. It's doubly bad, then, to be accused of the things you *haven't* done.)

Never mind that I had none of the other signs of being a meth addict; my skin, while not exactly in great shape, lacks the *huge fucking sores* you get while on meth. My face, while much slimmer in recent years, isn't skeletal. I'm sometimes a bit energetic, but I'm never tweaked-out twitchy. In short, calling me a meth user because I have bad teeth is about as valid as calling me a genius because I'm a fast reader.

This dentist had come to her decision, though, no matter what I said. She made a point of telling me that they didn't make dentures as discolored as I'd need and that I'd have to get used to having everyone see how dark my teeth were in comparison with these shiny white front teeth I'd have on the right side. She told me all this, with her poky metal shit in my mouth, and I wondered whether she was intentionally hitting the sore spots. I'm sure she dispensed actual medical advice at some point, but I stopped listening. Instead, I wondered whether she'd bother to take out all the bone fragments that needed removing or whether she'd just let them heal over and cause me trouble. I wondered how many people came back for this kind of idiocy.

So I had my surgery, got a denture plate in place of my front teeth, and never went back. Call it weakness, call it cowardice, it'd be true. There is a shred of dignity that I will not let go of. I will not intentionally put myself in that situation again.

And that's why I don't like dentists. I have never in my life felt more attacked, more vulnerable, trashier than I did in that dentist's chair. At least when people on the Internet call you a meth user, you can console yourself with the fact that these people are idiots, as evidenced by the fact that they have nothing better to do than cast aspersions at strangers online. When a dentist does it, drill in hand, it's impossible not to worry that maybe that person is a serial killer, and fuck that. Not doing it again. Not even risking it. And it's not like there's a huge pool of dentists out there who will treat someone like me on a payment plan. I can't just shop around until I find one with a decent bedside manner.

My denture from that surgery broke about two years later. It just snapped while I was trying to eat a hamburger, separating the plate that fits on the roof of my mouth from the actual visible teeth part. I superglued it together for a while, until it wore down around the raw edges and wouldn't fit properly. Now I just use a lot of dental paste and try to never consume anything in front of another human.

So that was kind of awful. Worse, my teeth are actually one of the things I can honestly say aren't my fault. My destroyed teeth are the result of a car accident nearly a decade ago, in which the other driver was drunk and high and had been busted for those things so many times they'd revoked his license. There was no question of liability.

I was in the passenger seat because I hate driving in cities and always let others take that honor if possible, and my jaw hit the dash so hard I exploded the airbag. Over time it became clear that I had nearly exploded my jaw along with it.

I had car insurance, sure, but it only covered liability and uninsured drivers. (Thank God for *that* extra five bucks in coverage a month!) I needed a car to get to work. So when the insurance company offered me a settlement check, I didn't think twice about signing the waiver (which, it turned out, meant that I had no right to future damages). I took it and bought another car. I didn't realize that check would be it—that there was no more money coming to take care of the damage the other driver had done to *me*. I thought they were just separate claims or something. I'd never filed a major insurance claim before; I had no idea what I was doing.

So that's how I found myself with a mouthful of fucked-up teeth and no resources to deal with them. Truthfully, even if I'd known what that waiver meant, I'm not sure that I'd have made a different decision. If it was a choice between my teeth and my car, I had to choose the car. I could survive with bad teeth, but I'd starve and lose my apartment without a car to get me to and from work. That said, I never would have imagined that dental care wouldn't be something I'd have access to for nearly a decade.

So I got the car (which turned out to be a lemon, *because of course it did*) and kept working, and over the years my teeth have continued to decay. I've brushed, flossed, rinsed religiously. And the cavities spread regardless. I bought a Waterpik. I bought made-for-TV mouth-cleaning tools.

Nothing helps.

My teeth are, since my story went viral, a thing I now talk about. But until the moment that I went full fuck-you gutterpunk and took them out for the whole Internet's viewing to underscore the effect of my dental problems, I hid them. I spent years learning to speak with my mouth closed, learning how to fake eat in public when I couldn't avoid it. I rarely told anyone when my mouth was hurting. It's not like I have an option now, but there's nothing that shames me more than acknowledging that I have failed at this too—this basic idea of keeping your own bones and enamel to yourself, of *having* them at all. Nothing is worse than eating in public, because I mostly can't eat with my broken denture in. I usually eat alone, at night, tearing off bits of food and bolting them down without chewing whenever my stomach tells me that it can't wait any longer. There is no joy in food for me anymore; it is a necessary evil, something I consume to stay alive but lacking in anything like taste or texture. I don't eat much.

I've lost a lot of weight. People keep asking me how I've done it, and I always wonder what I should say. Mostly, I tell them that it's just losing baby fat now that I am out of my twenties. Sometimes I seriously consider telling them that they really ought to try a nice strong periodontal disease (it does *wonders* for your thighs!).

I don't smile. Someone found a picture of me smiling from back in 2006, before my front teeth went and a wisdom tooth cracked off. It is one of the last times I smiled on camera, if not *the* last. I don't allow people to take my picture anymore because nobody can ever just take a picture. Everyone wants you to grin like an insane person. They will cajole and wheedle and bring the whole group photo to a screeching halt until you finally, shamefully, admit that you can't, that you don't want a picture of you like this to exist. Or you have to be an ass, irrationally angry about a seemingly innocuous request. That'll get you out of it too. I actually don't mind being in pictures and I wish I had more to remember my friends and milestones with, but I've spent the better part of a decade telling everyone that I have a huge aversion, that it's best not to ask or expect, because I don't want to deal with the inevitable "Smile!"

Actually, never smiling has had an interesting impact on my life. I can't repress laughing with my friends, the people who are safe, who can see a broken mouth and not notice it. But among people who don't know me, about half of my jokes fall flat, because I am not doing the human thing and grinning my way through, making clear that my dry observation is meant to be amusing rather than cutting. So I learned to stop telling jokes, because while I have a lively sense of humor, I can't properly express it with my face.

It even messes with my relationships. My husband, for obvious reasons, would like to kiss me. I, for obvious reasons, feel like kissing is the anti-sex; once I have been reminded that I have teeth, I cease feeling anything like alluring.

My teeth have become one of my most hated obsessions. I'm constantly reminding myself to keep my fucking mouth shut (which has its side benefits in that never shutting up has been a problem for me in my life) and to make sure my denture is adjusted properly so I don't have weird sunken-mouth lips. I have two broken-to-the-point-of-missing teeth that are visible on the right top side, and I use cotton wadding to cover that as far as the basic "something vaguely whitish that has mass" concerns. I worry at my teeth with my tongue, testing which are still sound enough to masticate should I be caught in a rare public eating situation. I take prophylactic ibuprofen so the swelling doesn't get out of control. There's no good way to predict the swelling, and once it's started, the pain isn't quite the worst, but your productivity is pretty much gone for the day. As soon as the swelling sets in, there isn't much you can do besides hold ice to your cheek and pray.

When I was in acute pain, before I learned better, I used to go to urgent care or the ER. A lot of urgent cares won't dispense painkillers. My guess has always been that they assume you're an addict or a seller. In the ER, I think they figure that the wait and the bills are enough to deter most abusers, so they'll give you a day or maybe two of real no-shit medicine to get you through a few days' work. To get any sort of actual medicinal regimen, you have to have an actual doctor, a general practitioner. I don't have time to chase down a doctor's appointment when I'm in pain.

So why, I am asked, have I simply not gone to one of the free dental clinics? Well, because they aren't exactly flinging their doors open. I've researched some programs, looking for anyone who could help. Sometimes I am too rich, because I have a job at all. Sometimes I live in the wrong county, and the grant providing the funds is restricted to residents of the next county. A few times I've been unable to take off enough time from work to make it to where the clinic is, much less to do it for the multiple visits required to complete the job. Twice I've been told that they don't do critical cases, only basic cleanings and fillings, both of which are laughably inadequate at this point. So I have carried on, hoping to get dental insurance at some point. What I refused to confront or articulate for years was that it was likely I'd simply wind up being one of those gross people with no teeth. Probably by the age of thirty-five.

But rationality rarely enters into health care. Mostly, at least for me, medicine has been a patchwork of what's around when I really can't avoid seeking care for a second longer. And most of my interactions with the health care industry have pretty much made me want to avoid it all the more from then on. ER visits usually involve waiting for hours and then being handed a couple of ibuprofen for my trouble. And the whole time I'm waiting for those ibuprofen, I get to wonder what the bill's going to come out to and whether I should stay and wait longer or just go home and hope for the best.

Look, I'm not stupid. I can *be* stupid, but I'm usually fairly savvy. I can read at a college level. I can do complex math problems given enough time and scratch paper. But I had trouble finding medical care.

Well, scratch that. I have had trouble finding *decent* medical care. It's why I didn't have prenatal care for my eldest daughter. I found out I was pregnant in October, days before the last election I ever worked on. I had a suspicion I was pregnant—I mean, that's why I'd peed on seven pregnancy sticks, all of which had turned out positive. But I couldn't bring myself to believe the results, since I'd been told so many times that it was practically impossible for me to get pregnant. I made a command decision that all those store-bought tests had to have been defective. So I went to the local Planned Parenthood and requested a blood test. But after the nurse heard about all the tests I'd already taken she just laughed and went straight for an ultrasound. Sure enough, within three seconds she told me that I was already six weeks gone.

I didn't think about the pregnancy much to begin with; I had a job to finish, then we'd sort out what to do next. I knew that I'd be facing weeks of unemployment after Election Day, and I could sort out prenatal and baby products and such then. The pregnancy prompted our decision to send my husband to school; we'd been thinking about it since he came home from Iraq, and it seemed as good a time as any to have a guaranteed income. The GI Bill, along with paying for tuition, pays a living stipend. It would just cover all of our expenses if we were careful. I could stay home with the baby until I was ready to go back to work, and then we'd be in a decent position until he graduated. The stipend wasn't so much that we wouldn't qualify for Medicaid, so the birth itself would be covered.

It didn't exactly go according to plan. First, we qualified for Medicaid, and I started looking for an OB. There weren't a ton of doctors accepting new Medicaid patients. Planned Parenthood doesn't do prenatal care. I found my clinic through a flyer, advertising that it did in fact accept Medicaid and was enrolling NOW! In the waiting room for my first appointment, I realized that I was at a faith-based clinic. It was a church ministry.

Now, normally I'm cool with the Jesus folks doing the poor-people tending. It's sort of their mandate, and I honestly do not care about the religious beliefs of anyone willing to make sure my kid gestates properly. But there are the charities that happen to be church-run, and then there are the church charities. I was at one of the latter. That distinction is important: Some ministries are set up by churches to provide a service, and some seem to be set up to proselytize, tacking the service on as an afterthought.

When I showed up, I was ushered into an office, where I did the initial paperwork and learned about all the things the woman helping me praised Jesus for. Her pencil didn't break, praise Jesus. The weather was decent, praise Jesus. I honestly do not know what was in the paperwork she was walking me through; I was much too fascinated by this person who was nearly finished with the third page, praise Jesus.

After that, I was taken to an exam room, where I was greeted by a lovely young woman who took my blood pressure and asked me if I had a church home. She was followed by a nurse who told me that Jesus had a plan for this baby and congratulated me on making the decision to bear it. I asked about maybe getting another ultrasound—my weird hormones and the sudden ability to bear children had me freaking out that this kid wasn't viable, and I was terrified of coming to terms with having a child only to discover that it wouldn't make it. But I was told that they only did ultrasounds in the third trimester unless there was a problem.

And that was the end of my appointment. No reassurance, no actual medical advice, no real exam. Just some routine tests and the clear message that Jesus wanted me to have this baby. I, certain that Jesus also wanted me to have an ultrasound and pretty sure that I could manage a pregnancy just as well without that sort of help, never went back. There didn't seem to be much point in returning to a place that gave no better advice than to drink a lot of water and not get into a hot tub, which were both helpfully bullet-pointed on the packet of papers they sent home with me.

I did take a few stabs at finding a different clinic. The ones with open spots didn't take Medicaid, and the ones that accepted Medicaid were full. So instead, I read a lot of books, called all of my old friends who had kids, and compulsively Googled things to find out whether they were normal or whether I should present myself at the ER. Eventually, I did just that when my daughter finally decided to arrive.

Any hospital in a large city is used to random pregnant women showing up to give birth. I think, though, that most of them have a doctor. They wanted to know who mine was, and I told them that I was pretty sure whoever was on call that night would be my doctor.

I actually don't remember most of the process. I was in a room, then another room, and I was kind of too busy being in labor to really care what was happening. Tom took care of the paperwork; we gave them the Medicaid card and that was pretty much it. Then I had a baby. I think the process was probably streamlined given that there was going to be a baby soon whether or not the paperwork was done, and they much preferred that I give birth in the birthing room instead of in the waiting room, where it would be rather hard to clean up afterward.

We were visited by social workers a lot in the next days. I don't know what all I filled out; they showed up at random times. If I was awake, they had me fill out paperwork. If I was asleep, they woke me and had me fill out paperwork. I'd failed to plan ahead and bring pay stubs with me, which the lady was kind of miffed about, so I had to bring those in later.

I've been called crazy. It's not untrue. I suffer from a syndrome called We Don't Know What the Fuck Your Damage Is. That is to say, I've been diagnosed with so many things that it's impossible to tell what's likely the real problem. I mean, clearly I struggle. Things that are simple for most people don't come naturally to me. I have trouble bending my will to anyone, including myself. I'm reckless and impulsive. I'm irrational and prone to anger when I am in certain moods, and those moods occur more frequently than you'd expect. I go through depressive phases, lasting days or months, and I can destroy my entire life through sheer inattention in three weeks flat, because even if you can't muster the energy or the will to open your mail, they still want the money for the bills. At times I'm an insomniac, and at others I can't get out of bed. None of these things are typically so bad for me as to be unmanageable, but managing them sometimes doesn't leave much room for anything else.

It's not like mental health clinics are thick on the ground, like the people who need their services. Being poor in and of itself is an aggravating factor in a lot of mental illnesses; the stress is pretty brutal. If you're already kind of fragile, it can be really rough. I won't say that a good clinic for poor people doesn't exist somewhere, but I've never found a mental health professional who was willing or able to deal with only the parts I needed to fix, the insomnia and paralysis and depression (at least some of which is situational, and I'll discuss that more in Chapter 4).

When I have sought treatment for these things, the professionals seem to only want to talk about my anger. They talk about my fatalism, my caustic outlook. They see these things as problems to be fixed. Personally, I think that anger is the only rational response to my world sometimes, but when you're asking for services, you don't get to pick what they treat you for. Either you agree with them or you're labeled uncooperative and kicked out of the program.

The last time I found myself really struggling and went in, they told me that I would have to spend hours in treatment each week. And that was the only option. It was either that or no treatment at all. So I chose the latter. Now, to be fair, I showed up in a right state. I was having a bit of a meltdown because I was terrible at my job and putting in too many hours to be failing that hard, and my husband was having a rough patch, and the kids were sick, and I had just realized again that this was it, this was life, this was how it was going to be until I died. The best I could hope for was that not all of these things would happen at once too often. I can see them thinking I was seriously this critical all the time.

I went to the clinic hoping that I could develop a relationship with a therapist who would then be able to prescribe me the drugs that have made me competent and invulnerable, the ones that stave off emotional disaster so that I can simply get through the crunch. Even at my most breakdowny, I generally realize that I am reacting irrationally. What I need from the mental health system that I have never been able to get is just enough support to maintain.

What I need, what would probably actually improve my life outcome, is someone who I can call, can see frequently for short stretches when I've hit a rough patch, and can then not call when I'm okay. Someone who knows my history and won't question it when I call and ask, apropos of nothing, for something to help me sleep or avoid panic attacks. I need someone who's worked with me for long enough to understand that I don't really like medicine and that if I'm asking, it's serious. In short, I need the kind of mental health support that many people with quality insurance take for granted.

When I've had the guts to see a doctor about an ailment, I haven't had the access, and when I've had the access, I haven't had the guts. Until quite recently, I was scared to death that if a doctor ever did find something really wrong with me, I'd be *completely* uninsurable, so I never went to the ER for anything that wasn't obvious and small, like a bad flu or potentially broken ankle.

Mostly, if I'm honest, I've been scared of the *look*. It's in doctor's offices and around social workers where I get the lectures, the judgments, the stares. People treat me like I'm a fucking idiot, as though I am incapable of noticing this rather large problem, rather than incapable of addressing it before it becomes such a large problem.

I came in for a fair bit of judgment over a cyst I developed. Doctors assumed I was just too ignorant to notice it, rather than the truth, which was that I lacked insurance and it wasn't life-threatening. I promise you, I was aware of the cyst I had for years. You can look up the gory details—it's called a pilonidal abscess. I think it's due to a tailbone injury I had as a teenager. A couple of times a year, my ass would swell and I'd smell like a rotting corpse for a few days in addition to the rather painful fact that I couldn't sit or stand in any position that didn't add to the pressure of the infection. It wasn't until just after my first daughter was born, when I had three months of Medicaid left, that I could have it excised. Prior to that, it landed me in the ER more than once, and every time, I'd be told patronizingly that I could simply have it taken care of, and probably should. Every time, I asked the doctor if they'd be willing to do the surgery at the rate I could afford; while I didn't have any takers, it did, at least, ensure that I didn't have to hear yet another explanation that surgery exists—as if it were something I'd never heard of simply because it was something I couldn't have.

Preventative medicine, man, it's a miracle. You can go to orthodontists and surgeons and eye doctors and rehab facilities after you throw out your back so that you don't wind up bedridden and debilitated. You get antibiotics and pain-killers and blood pressure medicine.

Seriously, vision care alone is a miracle that only happens to the rich, never mind the rest. They don't get deep fore-head wrinkles at thirty from spending their twenties squint-ing, they don't get headaches that cause them to take a large amount of ibuprofen every day—which, as all the bottles are pretty clear on, can't be good for you. They can see some-thing in the first second it comes into their field of vision instead of five seconds later. The glasses and the decent food and the orthodontists—all of those things require money.

There is a price point for good health in America, and I have rarely been able to meet it. I choose not to pursue treat-ment if it will cost me more than it will gain me, and my cost-benefit is done in more than dollars. I have to think of whether I can afford any potential treatment emotionally, financially, and timewise. I have to sort out whether I can afford to change my life enough to make any treatment worth it—I've been told by more than one therapist that I'd be fine if I simply reduced the amount of stress in my life. It's true, albeit unhelpful. Doctors are fans of telling you to sleep and eat properly, as though that were a thing one can simply do.

Now, I'm not saying the system doesn't work at all. I've

LINDA TIRADO

had lifesaving treatment, like when my throat swelled so much they had to put a tube in it to keep me breathing. I've got friends who can leave their houses only because they found a program to get them a wheelchair. Many people have needs that the system is built to meet, and it does that fairly efficiently to the extent that there's money.

The trouble is that we've left so many holes in the safety net Moby-Dick could swim through it. The system can't support everyone who needs the help, and it's led to a pastiche of half-finished treatments and conflicting diagnoses. We have the technology. Maybe we can start using it? There are a lot of us that would be awfully pleased to get some antibiotics.

4

I'm Not Angry
So Much as I'm
Really Tired

Almost nothing is more degrading than standing in a welfare line. The people who are looking at you know exactly how much money you make, because they know how poor you have to be to qualify. And the workers are either lovely or the worst human beings you'd ever care to meet. I had a caseworker who called just to check in because she knew I'd gotten a new job. And I had one who ignored me completely, just had me sit silently at her desk until she needed me to verify my information. Then she ignored me some more, and then she told me I could go. I left, with no idea what had just happened. I called the state to find out what changes she'd made to my file the next day rather than speak up during that incredibly effective stonewall.

I've felt the poorest with the people who were supposed to be helping me. I get that their jobs suck and they're overworked, but I go out of my way to not be another asshole customer. I have my paperwork and a list of questions ready to go. I have all my references, my pay stubs, medical bills, everything. Indexed. Sometimes I don't have a document, but then it's on my list of questions, to find out what I can use as a substitute. But often, none of that matters, because I am poor and asking for the benefits that I am qualified for and entitled to as a citizen, and in some people's eyes that makes me less than human.

Often enough, I *feel* less than human—or less than the human that I know myself to be. For example, I love to read. I'm a naturally curious person, apt to ask uncomfortable questions without realizing it because I just want to know something. But I don't read when I'm working at minimum wage or near it. I'm too tired. I fall asleep because the effort of moving my eyes across the page and processing information is simply too much; my brain won't allow me to use what little energy I have left on frivolities like self-improvement. It just wants me to stare blankly at a wall or flickering screen until I pass out.

Understand that when I say I am tired and in the same breath bitch about a lack of hours at work, it's because I'm counting the totality of the shit that I have to deal with while being poor. It is super-inconvenient, all the time.

There's one episode of my life in particular that was just the worst. I was working two jobs, with no car. I lived two miles from one job and three miles from the other. It wasn't an inhuman amount of mileage; some people run that for fun. But then afterward, some people go home and relax.

So I'd get up in the morning, walk to work at about five a.m., and wait tables from six to about noon. I'd be home by about one, at which point I'd pass out unless I had errands to run. Then I'd get up at six, shower and fix my hair for the bar, walk three miles, tend bar until one or two in the morning, and either beg a ride from a co-worker or walk home. I'd get home at two or three, unwind, take a short nap, and start all over again.

Now, nobody can maintain that forever, and if I'd been lucky enough to get that many hours, I'd have been doing okay. The problem was that both these jobs were weekends or prime eating-out days only—three or sometimes four days each. So I'd spend Monday recuperating from the weekend, Tuesday trying to find better work (which also required more than a few miles of walking around dropping off applications), Wednesday taking care of the house, and Thursday taking a spare shift from one or the other job.

In other words, my commuting time was comparable to a typical suburbanite's: one, maybe two hours. Except mine was on foot, and it was to jobs at which I was on my feet all day. It's why I've never felt much need to exercise; I spend hours each day lifting heavy things and bending into impossible positions to get through stockrooms. I've stood and repeated so many times that I can assemble a cheeseburger in twenty seconds flat, assuming it's got multiple toppings. Less, if it's simple. You get plenty of miles in while running around a retail store or factory floor.

So I was either working or walking to or from work, about sixty hours every week. How did I spend my remaining time? Well, remember that I was walking. I lived in a fairly central location, but it was just about a mile or two from anything I needed, like a grocery store or a Laundromat. I did laundry twice over the weekend because I could make my clothes last two shifts but not three, so that was six hours. I went grocery shopping once a week, so that was four hours. I slept, so that was around fifty. I spent eight hours or so every week looking for work locally. I went to the unemployment office once a week to check the job boards, and that was five hours. I generally picked up a spare shift on Thursdays, so that was another six or so. I showered at least twice a day, what with all the walking, so that was about seven hours a week gone to washing or drying myself. And that leaves about three hours a day for everything else.

I was always and forever dreading the next time I'd have to get off the couch. I would finally sit down, and I would realize that if I had any hope of waking up at a reasonable hour tomorrow, I really did have to be in bed in three hours, and the dishes still needed to be done, and the toilet needed to be scrubbed, and I'd promised someone I'd make them dinner because I owed them and they got sick and called in the favor.

When some wealthier people sense an unwillingness in lower-paid workers to move faster than they absolutely have to, or to do much of anything with their free time, it's because we are marshaling our resources. We're not lazy; we're stockpiling leisure while we can. I can't tolerate more mental exercise after a full day of logistics and worry. Full capacity just isn't an option.

We start the day with a deficit. Most poor people don't wake up feeling refreshed and rested. When I wake up in the morning, I'm in pain. If it's ragweed or wood-burning season, I wake up with insane headaches. If I'm spared that, there's still my aching back, stiff from a night on a mattress that was worn out long ago. There's not a moment in my life that my mouth doesn't hurt; my tongue is raw from touching broken teeth and my jaw isn't any happier about them. (I fully realize that some of the trouble is that I don't know how bad I feel. There's no baseline, no normal "healthy" to compare an average day with.)

I'm not trying to say that only poor people feel pain. The point here is that life is a bit peachier if you have medicine or are under a doctor's supervision to treat these things. Allergies are less severe if you get allergy shots. My headaches are partially due to my jaw-teeth trouble. I realize the aging process would suck enough on its own—I'm generally less than pleased to have it helped along on a daily basis because I don't have enough money to seek proper medical attention. For fuck's sake, a decent *mattress* can be considered a contributor to an optimal health outcome.

But poor people wake up knowing that today, no matter how physically shitty we may feel, we can't call in sick or slack off at our desk surfing the Internet. We have to go to our crappy jobs no matter what. We will feel guilty about the bills and the dishes and we will firmly put them out of our mind as we march out the door in our polyester uniform shirts. Or worse, we will have to find something to do with our endless unemployed hours.

Sometimes, that's all the day is, just another gray nothing. Other times, it's already a bad day and people just have to fucking push me. I've got a bit of a temper, and I have trouble holding my tongue when I'm pretty sure someone's being an asshole. My record from waking up to losing it is in the neighborhood of an hour. Mostly I make it through a whole day, but sometimes it's just not in the cards. The night before my record-setting morning, I'd made it home from work at ten p.m. and passed out by eleven. I'd been working extra and was short on sleep to begin with. My boss called at five a.m. wanting me to come in. I drank some coffee and dragged my sorry ass out the door, and when I showed up, he was mad that it had taken me half an hour to come in. He'd been under the impression that when I said, "I'll be there," I meant that I'd use my teleportation device instead of the beater car I had at the time. I blew it off, figuring that he was just in a bad mood. But he simply couldn't let it go—every time someone complained about this or that setup not being done properly, he said that if only I'd been there on time we'd have made it.

I lost it. Completely. This is the version of what I said that I can best remember through my blistering rage: "If you think I'm so goddamned terrible, why did you call me in? Did you not realize that I'd be on a fourteen-hour shift and that I was running on a few miserable fucking hours of sleep? WHAT IS WRONG WITH YOU, YOU INCOMPETENT FUCKING ASSHOLE?" And I said all this in my outdoor voice. In front of customers. I spent the afternoon looking for work, as I was newly unemployed.

Being poor is something like always being followed around by violins making "tense" movie music. You know that commercial where the band Survivor follows a guy around playing "Eye of the Tiger"? Yeah, it's like that, but the musicians are invisible and they're playing the shower scene from *Psycho*. Nobody likes being harried, but for a lot of us it starts upon waking and doesn't let up until we crash at night. Eventually, you just know that something bad is going to happen. That's not paranoia or pessimism; it's reality.

When my story went viral, I got a lot of blowback from people demanding to know how I dared to have children while I was living in a weekly motel. Well, I'll tell you: That's not how we started out the pregnancy. The VA didn't end up paying us the living stipend that we'd expected so we'd gotten a cheap apartment. That was fine, for the short term. Until one day, when I was heavily pregnant, a summer storm flooded our apartment and destroyed everything we owned.

The landlord hadn't paid for proper maintenance on the storm drains, and they backed up. We didn't have family in the area, so we went to stay at the motel while we sorted out the damage. We'd been in touch with maintenance, who'd assured us that they'd take care of the water.

What we hadn't realized was that the landlord's version of "taking care of it" was having the guys run a Shop-Vac for a while and then set up some box fans. This was to take care of a flood that was feet deep. The water soaked into the concrete walls so thoroughly that when we stopped in a few days later, you could see the mold growing to above your head.

We didn't have enough money to pay for both the motel and our rent. We called the landlord to get a new apartment, maybe one that wasn't toxic, and were told that the apartment was fine now that it was dry. We called the health department and the press, neither of whom cared much. The health department guy, in all fairness, happened to not be in charge of this particular issue and couldn't tell me who was. But he agreed that we definitely shouldn't live there, especially not with a baby.

The result? The landlord sued for eviction because we weren't paying the rent on our flooded apartment. Cue the movie violins. Something as simple as a summer storm can mean disaster. So I learned to simply expect that if things felt like they were going rather too well, something would come along to knock me back into reality.

Gruff attitudes are rife among people with low-wage jobs. And it's no wonder, really, considering the lives we lead. Yet many of our employers actually seem to think it's reasonable to require unfeigned good cheer in their employees, and this I don't get. It doesn't make sense to hire people at wages that guarantee they'll be desperate and then be disappointed when they're not always capable of pretending otherwise. Look, I don't like walking into a gas station or fast-food joint or box store and dealing with a bunch of sullen idiots either. But people don't seem to stop to wonder why we're uniformly so pissed off and unhelpful. I think you'll find that the happier employees are in general, the happier they are at work. It isn't rocket science. My guess is that, like me, a huge number of poor people are depressed. Anger is one of the few emotions that can penetrate depression. It's strong enough to punch through the haze, so a whole lot of people like me hold on to our anger. We cherish it. The alternative, at least for me, is a sort of dreary nothing. Anger and depression make for a cute couple, right?

Regardless of our mood, we're never fully checked into work because our brains are taken up with at least one and sometimes all of the following: 1) calculating how much we'll make if we stay an extra hour, 2) worrying we'll be sent home early because it's slow and theorizing how much we will therefore lose, 3) placing bets on whether we will be allowed to leave in time to make it to our other job or pick up our kids. Meanwhile, we spend massive amounts of energy holding down the urge to punch something after the last customer called us an idiot. People don't have any compunction about insulting service workers, but it's amazing how quickly they'll complain about your attitude if you're not sufficiently good-natured about it.

Our jobs are as much emotional labor as they are physical. What they are not, what they are never allowed to be, is mentally engaging. So we're trying to zombie out to survive. We're not allowed to deviate from policy even if the policy is kind of stupid and counterproductive. Nobody is interested in our thoughts, opinions, or the contributions we might be able to make—they want robots.

Our survival mechanisms are the things that annoy the

customers most. Next time you see someone being "sullen" or "rude," try being nice to them. It's likely you'll be the first person to do so in hours. Alternatively, ask them an intelligent question. I used to come alive when someone legitimately wanted to know what I'd recommend. I knew everything about my products, having stared at all the boxes while I restocked them, but people rarely wanted me to tell them about anything more than the price.

What's guaranteed to be counterproductive for you is demanding better service with a superior attitude. We'll perform better service. But we'll be sure to hand you the shirt that we know is stained, or the meat that's within the technical limit of servable but will probably taste less than optimal. And we'll do it with a shit-eating grin on our face and well-wishes on our lips, just like you demand but refuse to pay a single extra penny for.

If you want us to be happy to serve you, make it worth our while and be pleasant. Next time you're in a low-wage place, try walking up to an employee and saying, "I'm sorry to disturb you, I know you have work, but could you tell me where this thing I need is?" I guarantee you, *that* is how you get service from a demoralized staff. Respect their workload. There is no low-wage employer in the world that doesn't expect a ton of chores finished in a shift besides customer service. Don't just expect that millions of people are by nature pleased to grovel at the feet of your twenty dollars.

Humans in general aren't built that way, and Americans in particular. We're supposed to have a stubborn streak of pride, remember?

In Cincinnati, I lived just under two miles from the closest grocery store that carried the sort of formula my daughter could tolerate. She was insanely colicky, so I used to spend my free time walking her around the city, letting the vibration of the stroller lull her into farting an incredible amount before she finally, blessedly, fell asleep. I went to the store most days, buying only what we absolutely needed, because I couldn't fit much more in the stroller. I still love to wander, because if nobody knows where I am, then nobody can ask me for anything or call me about an unpaid bill. And I get angry out of all proportion when someone disturbs my peace, because it is so rare that I actually feel light and free.

I don't get much of my own time, and I am vicious about protecting it. For the most part, I am paid to pretend that I am inhuman, paid to cater to both the reasonable and unreasonable demands of the general public. So when I'm off work, please feel free to go fuck yourself. The times that I am off work, awake, and not taking care of life's details are few and far between. It's the only time I have any autonomy. I do not choose to waste that precious time worrying about how you feel. Worrying about you is something they pay me for; I don't work for free. You don't get to demand this ten minutes from me too. This is mine, and my family's.

I actually don't mind, on feminist grounds, when men tell me to smile. I can see why women would, but I've worked in bars and I've worked in strip clubs and I've learned that you can commodify anything, including sex and pretend love and faked respect and false empathy. "Smile," coming from a man, is just the opening chatter to me at this point. It is a sign that this particular man has nothing original to say and is probably kind of a dick.

I do mind the smile-on-command directive on class grounds. Listen here, buster. It's not my fucking job to decorate your world, not unless you're willing to make it so. Sure, I'll smile. That'll be five bucks.

I feel bad about my reactions sometimes, because I can't always stop them even when they're directed at someone who's having the same sort of day as I am. I was once at a store and could not for the life of me find the fucking diapers. I wandered the length and breadth of the place—nothing. I was exhausted, completely finished. Some poor woman who worked there stepped into my field of vision. I meant to ask where the diapers were stocked like a normal human being. What came out instead was "Why did you people hide the fucking diapers?" I couldn't tell you how that made it from brain to mouth. It just happens sometimes. So when I am on the receiving end of customers' misery, I'm never sure whether to actually be mad at the customers. Maybe they tried to be polite and just didn't have the energy, because when they were at work, someone else came in, and so on, and so on, and so on.

Maybe it's because, as I mentioned earlier, I spend a lot of the time depressed. Always have, always will. Give me medicine, I get less upset about being depressed, but the fact of it never leaves. Sometimes I am clinically, trouble-getting-out-of-bed depressed. Other times, I am just low-level, drag-myself-through-my-day depressed. Some people might call me pessimistic because I always expect disaster to occur. But looking at my life, I think that's bull. When I expect doom? That's what I call reality.

Mostly, I ignore the depression. I developed a caustic sense of humor. I discovered mosh pits to vent. I listen to seriously angry music. When that doesn't work, I soothe the emptiness with terrible food and old jazz. If that doesn't work and I can afford it, I go in and see someone about getting some medicine for a few weeks. That means making appointments any place I think I might be able to get in, assuming that I'll be turned down for service, and showing up to them all until I find someone who's willing to do me a solid and give me a week or two of anti-anxiety medicine. If I can't find anyone to do that, I just sort of check out for a while.

Those times, I can't get past the part of the day where you're supposed to put on pants. I'll stare at the pants. I will tell myself to put on the pants. I will get stern with myself about them. And then I'll lose a few hours to a discussion with myself about how much I actually really do deserve all the punishments I will heap upon me if I do not put on the pants. When I zone back in again, the sun will be down and it will blessedly be time for bed again.

Sometimes I can convince my boss that I have a terrible flu. Sometimes I just don't show up, and those times it's half and half whether I've got a job to go back to; it depends on how understaffed they are. Sometimes I haven't been employed in the first place.

Not all poor people are chemically depressed, but a lot of us are situationally depressed at any given time. And that's because our lives are depressing. I realize that might at first sound simplistic, but I don't think it's a lot more complicated than that.

When I think of myself and all the poor people I know, there is only one person who I would have called irrepressibly sunny. Her name was Melissa, and she seemed indefatigable. Nothing, and I mean not eviction, not being without electricity, not being called names—nothing brought this woman down. She once told me that even when she felt terrible, she liked being a bright spot. I'd known her for six months when her kid got in trouble and the school intimated that it was because she wasn't doing enough for him. And that's what finally broke her. She got into a terrible funk, withdrawn and silent unless you forced something out of her. She started noticing all the things that were wrong in her world, and that was the end. She was one of us.

That's the worst, watching someone lose hope. I'm not swelled with it personally, but I always like to see people who aren't only pretending to be in a good mood, people who are truly optimistic about life. Those people are contagious, even to a curmudgeon like me. It's heart-wrenching to watch that fade, like watching a star die or something. I can't think of anything poetic and tragic enough to describe it.

I recognize that the attitude that I fall into—hell, that I cultivate—as a ward against the instability of being poor isn't always helpful to me. But it's not as if I can just go in and out of it, like putting on or taking off my makeup. The attitude I carry as a poor person is my armor, and after so many years of fighting and clawing and protecting myself and my family from impending disaster, that armor has become a permanent part of me.

Take a walk through any impoverished neighborhood. You will hear the word "pussy" a lot. A lot. It's just how some people talk. "Suck my dick," a man will say jauntily to his friends. Or angrily to his friends. Or randomly to women passing on the street. "Fucking pussy" is a popular phrase too, as in "you're a" or "I need some." Street cant isn't something that poor Americans came up with magically a year after the Pilgrims got here. It's a product of environments in which everyone's always posturing just a bit, just in case. A lot of times it means absolutely nothing.

But there is always the potential that as you are walking down the street, some sort of altercation will erupt within feet of you. Maybe someone is angry with a cashier because their card was declined, and they start yelling about disrespect and ass-kicking and what they ought to do. Maybe a homeless person will loudly and suddenly commence complaining about whatever it is that is bothering them that day. Maybe a mercurial couple will have a disagreement in their own attention-seeking fashion.

I was sitting in a Denny's recently, drinking coffee and trying to finish writing a chapter of this book. The table next to me had a few kids, two men and a woman, all under twenty. And the table behind me had two people in it, one of whom took it into his head that he'd been insulted by Table 1 somehow. Next thing you know, everyone's out of their seats throwing insults back and forth, tossing gauntlet after gauntlet, trying to goad a fight. I wound up taking the aggressive dude outside to smoke while we waited for his friend to grab their food and leave. Someone else talked down the people who really had been confronted for zero reason.

That was a random Tuesday. I've been to the same Denny's more than once, and I expect to just drink my coffee. But you never know when you're going to be talking down an idiot. It doesn't happen all the time, and it's not like most trips to the store aren't rather boring and mundane. It's just that it *could* happen at any time in the environments where everyone is always tense and worried and stressed. It *does* happen with some frequency. And it's best to be prepared for the eventuality.

Being poor in the country requires a toughness. We have to be capable of changing our own damned tires and putting shims on a starter. We chop wood and catch or grow food. Country poor is not even going to the thrift store, because it's miles away. It's getting up and dealing with the animals and the crops (if you have them) before you go to work. It's expecting at any moment to break down at the side of the road because your truck is so old it doesn't have a computer in it anywhere. And there's no public transportation in the country. If you don't have a working car, you're hoofing it. Rain or snow.

So yeah, out of necessity poor people walk around being just a bit rough and tumble, a bit sharp-edged. We proudly declare that we are rednecks, we wear boots and have weapons with which to defend ourselves and we are doing well enough on our own, thank you. Or we scream that we are from streets somewhere, that we will take no shit, that our neighborhood doesn't have a place for weakness in it and it makes us hard like warriors.

It also makes me say "fuck." A lot. It's my vernacular as a matter of habit, and I developed it as a defense mechanism. Saying "fuck," especially as a woman, is the quickest and easiest way to assert that you aren't to be fucked with, or at least that you're pretending well enough. It's a tough word, a vulgar word, something you don't say comfortably if you're scared of public disapprobation or muggers.

That's the upside of it for me. The downside is that it doesn't go over well when it slips into situations where it's inappropriate and it might even come across as threatening. I know this affects how I'm treated when I engage with the upper classes, but it's a habit that's practically subconscious.

I walk with a tiny swagger. Many people who have lived in the not-so-nice parts of cities do this to varying degrees because it tells people from a distance that we know how to handle ourselves, and that we are streetwise enough to make a challenging target. It's also unconscious in me at this point. To middle- and upper-class people, it's one more thing that sets me apart, that sends the unintended signal that I don't belong in nicer company.

My tough demeanor was at first something I cultivated as a survival mechanism. But after a while it became more natural. It's a lot like hiding my teeth—I got so good at it that I didn't notice after a while. I stopped noticing anything, stopped registering things as inappropriate or odd. And I stopped noticing when I was being inappropriate or odd, to the extent that I ever knew.

Looking back, I can see where the crossing of the ways happened. I started to lose contact with the middle class at the same time that I became comfortable in the lower one. You can bridge both worlds, but only if you're consciously doing it and you're not too tired. Otherwise you revert. I'm perfectly capable of holding an intellectually stimulating discussion like a human being. But my friends will tell you that they can tell how tired I am by how frequently I replace polite words and phrases with profane or aggressive ones.

And I don't just have problems with playing the part of someone who gives a shit about the niceties; I have difficulty looking the part. That costs money.

I'm not going to claim that I had sterling self-esteem before I started seeing my economic status written all over my unmoisturized face. I was an awkward, overweight kid who liked books and chess. I was a nerd who missed the makeup and fashion years. But being poor sucked right out of me what little self-regard I might have had. Rich people complain when they have bad hair days or fat days. I have "fryer grease in my hair" days, and "not a single article of clothing makes me look like anything but shit" days. I'm not even going to bother explaining how bad teeth and bad skin might also get you pegged as less valuable, less worthy of respect. You're reading a book voluntarily, you're smart enough to figure it out. But those are only the *big* visible markers. There are a whole lot of small ones. If the average rich person had to walk around for a day wearing a polyester work uniform, they'd need Xanax.

Poverty, or poor, or working class—whatever level of not enough you're at—you feel it in a million tiny ways. Sometimes it's the condescension, sometimes it's that you're itchy. I don't think people who have never been poor quite understand that.

I like to use jeans as an example. I just bought my first decent pair, the exorbitant $70 kind. It's like some kind of fucking miracle. I didn't know denim wasn't supposed to be uncomfortable. And I'd heard about jeans making your butt look amazing, but I'd never believed it. The kind you can buy at Walmart come in two styles: mom jeans and low-cut skinny jeans meant for middle schoolers because no grown woman could get into them. Regardless of style, they are heavy, the fabric is the rugged we-mine-coal thickness, and once they stretch across your unfortunate lower abdomen, you're fucked. They'll hide the curves you like and prominently display the ones you'd rather nobody noticed.

Assuming, of course, that they fit at all. I have one favorite pair of jeans, which I've had for so long that they've gone soft from washing. I've worn them when I was a size 12 and when I was a size 16. If I wash them in really hot water and then throw them in a hot dryer, they'll shrink enough that I can belt them to stay up when I'm skinny. And if I wash them in cold and stretch the waistband while they're drying, they'll expand enough that I can zip them when I'm on the top side of my usual range of sizes. So yeah, when I put them on, I am wearing pants, but they're the kind that make you look weirder than you would just leaving the house without any pants on in the first place. At least if you're pantsless you're given the room to be crazy. Bad pants just mean bad taste for most people.

I'd never had occasion to walk into a makeup store until recently, when I was going on camera and desperately needed something for my face. I figured that if I went to a special makeup place, they could help me choose foundation and maybe lipstick, because I never know what color to get. The salesperson not only helped me with that, but she also hooked me up with free makeup application lessons, and gave me more free shit than I could have imagined. Samples of this, samples of that, here try this face cream. Just because I walked in with twenty bucks. It's insane, the perks you get at specialty stores.

I've heard my whole life that I should spend wisely, invest

in my appearance, that it will make people take me more seriously. Buy a few key pieces, the style authorities say, which would be great if I could ever scrape together $300 of disposable income to spend on a suit. A $20 bottle of makeup, okay, I can do that every now and then. I've got $50 sometimes, but it's still not enough to buy a suit with. If I could put away $20 a week in a little piggy bank marked "nice suit for Linda," then I'd have enough to buy it about fifteen weeks from now. And who am I kidding? By the time I have $40 saved, I can think of ten other things that $40 could be spent on. Stuff like milk and toilet paper. How often am I really going to wear a suit, and how important might that suit be the one time I need it?

More than once I've shown up to a professional event wearing something entirely inappropriate. I've gone too casual to formal events, and I've gone the other way too. I'll show up to a casual event in heels. I don't have the time or resources for style handbooks and fashion magazines, and I don't get the social cues and niceties. And even if I did get them, I couldn't afford them.

Let me clarify: I'm not saying that all poor people don't know how to dress. There are certainly those among us who do better than others in this area (we have our share of aspiring fashion designers who watch *Project Runway* and all those makeover shows, and you can learn to put on any kind of eye shadow in the world on YouTube). But even if I knew what to wear, I couldn't afford it. I once wore a suit two sizes too small because I'd gained some weight and didn't have anything else that fit. It didn't occur to me until hours into the thing that the only people speaking seriously with me were men looking for company that evening. What I actually had to say was never heard. Then there was the black-tie event to which I wore a light summer dress. Of course I knew it was the wrong season for it, but it was the nicest thing I had. I wasn't taken particularly seriously at that event either.

So, if first impressions are as important as everyone says they are, what do you think my chances are of getting a professional job if I'm competing against someone who dresses the part? I guarantee you that even if that other job candidate is a little less qualified than me, the boss is going to feel more comfortable hiring the person who she's not afraid will stick out like a (poor) sore thumb at the weekly meeting with the CEO.

I didn't really realize that I was fully lower class in both sensibilities and presentation until I found myself at what was the last of my professional social engagements. I was attempting to resurrect something like a career during the worst part of our stay in Ohio, when we weren't getting our GI Bill stipend, and I thought maybe I could scrape something up. I was invited out to dinner by a bunch of old political work colleagues, and I found myself with nothing to say. I had no insights on the new restaurants or movies or bars, nothing that you typically reach for to make conversation. Every single addition I could have made would have been inappropriate: I couldn't have talked about my neighbor getting in a fight with his truck while he was drunk because it wouldn't start and he thought punching it might help. (His roommate had disabled the thing. Friends don't let friends drink and drive, and smart friends let friends punch the truck instead of them.) I couldn't talk about which food banks were best for produce and which for diapers. I also didn't order any food or drinks, which was pointed out repeatedly by the waiter. ("Are you *sure* you won't be ordering? Can I tempt you with this/that/the other?") I finally had to leave the table, track him down, explain that I couldn't afford anything on the menu, and ask could he *please* stop making a huge deal out of it? And after that, I never called any of those colleagues again. Nor did they call me.

I understand why that happened. But what I don't understand is why people who walk into a fast-food restaurant often seem to think I should put on the same smile and elegant demeanor they could expect at Saks or the bank where they put their money. I think the sorts of people who honestly think that service workers should be more smiley and gracious just don't get it. They don't get it because they can take so much for granted in their own lives—things like respect, consideration, and basic fairness on the job.

Benefits. Insurance. They're used to the luxury of choosing the most aesthetically pleasing item on the shelf, of caring what color their car is rather than simply whether it runs or not. They don't understand how depressing it is to be barely managing your life at any given moment of the day. So forgive me if I don't tell you to have a pleasant day with unfeigned enthusiasm when I hand you your fucking hamburger. You'll have to settle for the fake sort.

In my world, we don't have the time or the energy to bullshit about our feelings or worry about anyone else's. When I've found myself in professional situations, I'm driven nearly to distraction by how much fucking effort is wasted making sure we all feel nice and fuzzy and comfortable. I don't get that; it's not part of work to me. And it keeps me from getting ahead. If someone asks me my opinion on something, I simply give it. I don't bother spending five minutes talking about the weather and how lovely your shirt is first. I am thinking about the question I was asked. I figure nobody's getting paid to win the office nice competition. And it's amazing to me that some of the same people who can walk by a homeless person without even blinking are obsessed with what everyone thinks of them at work. Meanwhile I know that if I wasted half as much time in my service jobs talking about my feelings as I have in my professional life, I'd be out of work and lying right next to that homeless guy my white-collar friends just skirted past.

Maybe feelings are something that only professional people are allowed to have. My friends and I know that no one gives a shit about ours. We're constantly told to know our place and not make a fuss about the insane conditions we're expected to deal with, both at home and at work. And yeah, this discussion about attitude is coming back to the subject of work a lot, because guess what? It's what we spend a huge percentage of our lives on. And how we're treated there isn't something we can just shake off when we leave. It becomes a part of us, just like that armor we wear.

But still we're told to keep smiling, and to be grateful for the chance to barely survive while being blamed for not succeeding. Whether or not that's actually true isn't even relevant; that's what it feels like. Unwinnable. Sisyphean.

Responsible poverty is an endless cycle of no. No, you can't have that. You can't do that, can't afford that, can't eat that, can't choose that. This is off-limits, and that is not for you, and this over here is meant for different kinds of people. More than once I've spent money I couldn't really afford simply to state that I *could*, if only to myself. Just to say it.

To be told that you deserve nothing more than that, are entitled to nothing more, is enraging. If poverty is supposed to be like prison, then why don't we kill two birds with one stone and put prisoners in all the low-wage jobs? All the private prisons would be wildly profitable, and the poor people would deserve their poverty because it would be their punishment.

Sure, we can beat the odds. Sometimes we can climb out of it. You're reading this book by a service worker, after all. But the irony of my success here is that I didn't get this chance because I worked my balls off for some asshole who thought me ungrateful for my sub-living wage. You're reading this book by me because lightning struck, because my story went viral. And by definition, that can't happen for everyone. You can hope for your one real shot, but you sure as hell don't plan for it. It hurts too much to plan and plan again and keep waiting for the magic day.

So that's been my American dream. And it's reality for millions of us, the people who are looking grumpy behind the counter. Our bodies hurt, our brains hurt, and our souls hurt. There's rarely anything to smile about.

5

I've Got Way
Bigger Problems
Than a Spinach
Salad Can Solve

We all cope in our own special ways. I smoke. My friend drinks. In fact, I'm highly confident in betting that you and many of your friends cope by drinking as well. Come home from a long day at work, and what do you do? Pop open a beer? Or a bag of potato chips? Or maybe you take a Valium when you're feeling stressed out. Or get a massage. Or go to your gym and sit in the sauna room.

Why are other people's coping mechanisms better than poor people's? Because they're prettier. People with more money drink better wine out of nicer glasses. And maybe they get a prescription for benzos from their own personal on-call psychiatrist instead of buying a pack of cigarettes. They can buy whatever they like and it's okay, because retail therapy is a recognized course of treatment for the upper classes. Poor people don't have those luxuries. We smoke because it's a fast, quick hit of dopamine. We eat junk because it's cheap and it lights up the pleasure centers of our brain. And we do drugs because it's an effective way to feel good or escape something.

I get that poor people's coping mechanisms aren't cute. Really, I do. But what I don't get is why other people feel so free in judging us for them. As if our self-destructive behaviors therefore justify and explain our crappy lives.

Newsflash: It goes both ways. Sometimes the habits are a reaction to the situation.

And now I have to add one big caveat: Sometimes, sure, the stupid shit we do does explain our crappy lives. Are there meth addicts out there from nice middle-class homes who ended up homeless and far worse off than I've ever been? Absolutely. And if you want to believe that addiction is a person's fault and not a disease, then you can go right on ahead and judge that person for having brought about his own downfall.

But unless you're prepared to convince me that smoking and smoking alone keeps me poor, then please, spare me the lecture. I know it's bad for me. I'm addicted, not addled. There are reasons that I smoke, and they're reasonable ones. They keep me awake, they keep me going. Do they poison my lungs and increase my chances of getting cancer? Obviously. Does that stop me? No. Because the cost-benefit isn't a simple *I like it* versus *I'll possibly live longer*. It's *I will be able to tolerate more* versus *I will perpetually sort of want to punch something*.

I once talked to a neighbor about the fact that people who lived on our block were statistically likely to die earlier than the people who lived five blocks over in the wealthy neighborhood. He told me that it was just life, it was the way it was. He'd stopped questioning it. So if you already figure you're going to die early, what's the motivation for giving up something that helps get you through the here and now?

Look, I'm not saying that getting in a cage match or smoking copiously and with glee is exactly good for my longevity. But I don't much see the point in worrying about the end of my life if stress will kill me first. If I don't vent, don't perform some kind of self-medicating, there won't be an old age anyway. I'll wind up dead or in jail or institutionalized when I finally lose it.

Let me be clear: I am not all poor people. Of course there are wholesome people in every class. There are poor people who would never dream of doing anything as déclassé as using drugs. This whole book could be called *You Can't Put an Entire Third of the Country into One Group of Behaviors*.

Often, those folks who are unlike me are religious. I tend to think of religion as the same sort of thing as smoking—a soothing ritual that brings someone a moment of peace. But if I don't want to be judged for my habits, I'm sure as hell not going to judge anyone else for theirs. That's why I always defend religious people against those assholes who act like they're too good for anything so magical as religion. We all think magically about something.

So, on the one hand, sure, poor people have been known to engage in some unhealthy behaviors. It's not as though we, the unwashed masses, are doing anything that *everyone* doesn't do. It's not like drug and alcohol and cigarette sales just stop once a consumer hits $75,000 a year in income or something. It's a bit galling, actually, to be lectured about my self-destructive habits by someone who's fighting his own hangover. You're still getting drunk, friends, whether enjoying a bottle of Bordeaux or drinking a can of Mickey's. But it seems that the disapprobation of excessive drinking is meant mostly for those of us on the rotgut end of the scale.

I think the reason for this is that people are less moralistic about the vices themselves than they are about the cost of the vices. The logic is that if you've got excess money and throw it away on booze and cigarettes, then that's your business. But if you're poor, then that's a sin and a shame. Because if you're poor, rich people assume you're on welfare, or you're getting food stamps or some other social services. Once you take a penny from the government, a morality clause goes into effect, where you're never allowed to have anything that you might actually enjoy. It's the hair shirt of welfare.

I have trouble understanding why taking a few grand a year in food stamps is somehow magically different than taking trillions as a bailout. Food stamps cost $76.4 billion for 2013, compared with trillions, possibly hundreds of those, for the banks. And that's just *one* instance of handouts for the upper parts of society; it's not like the feds handed cash to the banks and the rich are otherwise left to muddle on alone in the wilderness.

I do not see a difference, the way many people do, in the federal money. Whether you are getting your benefits in the form of SNAP cards or deductions, it's the same thing. There is this money that you otherwise would not have had, that the government gives you. Stimulus spending can happen in proactive or passive ways; whether it's a block grant or a tax break, it's still the government investing money in a thing because it wants to ease some burden for someone somewhere or to encourage or discourage certain behaviors. It wants people to not starve? Food stamps. It wants people to buy houses? Interest deductions.

The one difference? Rich people get way more from the government than poor people do—see above-referenced mortgage interest, capital gains, light inheritance taxes, retirement savings breaks—but the poor are the only ones getting shamed for it. You want to know how I could justify relaxing sometimes while I was on benefits? The same way you justify blowing a reckless amount of money on a really nice dinner while you take a business deduction because you talked about work for ten minutes.

People bitch about double taxation, where corporations are taxed for their profits and then they give money to their shareholders, who are also taxed. This is apparently hugely unfair, and the only reasonable solution is apparently to exempt people from having to pay taxes on their dividends. Because some kinds of income just don't count as income? Because someone, somewhere, already paid a tax on this particular individual dollar? By the same logic, I shouldn't be asked to pay payroll taxes because my bosses already paid taxes on it too.

Capital gain, by definition, is money you make for the simple fact of having money. That's it. No work, no nothing. Just have some money, wait for it to grow, and then you have more money. Which you clearly should not have to pay taxes on, because that would be unfair. Somehow.

This, of course, is nothing like unemployment, where an employer pays a tax for every employee, and then if I pull unemployment, I have to pay tax on that as well. But sure, keep thinking that we've got all the cushy non-taxation going on down here in the lower classes.

All humans chase good feelings. It's just that people with money chase them in ways specific to the upper classes, which makes it okay. You can't argue that a pair of expensive shoes or an expensive steak is actually something you need. It's just something that makes you feel good.

According to a study published in *Science* magazine, which is a place I trust about science things, your brain actually has less capacity when you're poor. The theory is that so much of your brain is taken up with poverty-related concerns that there's simply less bandwidth available for other things, like life. It's not the only study like that.

At Princeton, they've found that the effect on the brains of poor people from the stress about money alone is equivalent to losing a bunch of IQ points. And they've also found that if you remove the stress, our brains snap back and perform at the same levels you'd expect to see in a wealthier test-subject pool. The same goes for the short-term memory impairment and trouble with complexities—skip a night of sleep and tell me how well you're performing the next day; you'd be functioning on about the same level we do every day. We're not dumb—we're conserving energy.

They're even starting to find similarities between people in poverty and soldiers with PTSD.

Poor people didn't need to wait for the science to know this, though. We feel it. We could have told you that being always tired and distracted wasn't great for higher cognitive activity. I stopped thinking in higher concepts, gradually. I feel stupid when I realize how long it's been since I thought about anything beyond what I had to get through to keep everything moving along: no philosophy, no music, no literature. We know we're not at capacity, and it rankles. So we fix it, as best we can. I know a few veterans, dealing with mild to moderate cases of PTSD, who have turned into potheads. It keeps them from getting too jumpy, keeps their memories from being too sharp. I hear that bankers like coke to stay focused. College kids take Ritalin to study.

I flirt with addiction, drinking too much coffee and smoking too much, but I've never let myself go there because I think it'd be too much of a relief and I'd never be able to come back voluntarily. And if I were dragged back, I'd face a lifetime of having to say no to one more thing that I knew would make me feel good. I doubt I'd do well with that. I'm not particularly strong that way.

Self-medication is a thing that exists. We fake rest and nutrition like we fake everything else to make it through the day. Mostly, we do it with chemical assistance. I smoke because it keeps me calm, because it keeps me awake, because it keeps me from feeling hungry, because it gives me five minutes to myself, because it just feels good and I like it.

Have you ever felt tempted to go to one of those places where you can pay to smash china? I never have, but then I never saw a reason to pay to smash things. I just did it. It feels good, really good, to break things when you're frustrated. It doesn't actually solve anything, but for a second you feel better. I like breaking glass. It's therapeutic. It was my favorite part of working as a picture framer; we had to smash the flawed glass into tiny bits for disposal. More than once, I popped in to help on my day off just to smash things. It's the same logic that explains mosh pits.

One day, when I have nothing but free time, I will start a mosh pit for old people. I quit jumping into them only when I started to realize that I'd become the creepy old person in the corner. For years, though, mosh pits were my anger therapy of choice.

Sex is also therapeutic when it's blissfully mindless. Orgasms for orgasms' sake. It makes your muscles relax, your headaches lessen. It makes the stress go away for however long it lasts. It's kind of amazing to have some outlet, somewhere, that you don't have to work for; that's the whole point of having a fuckbuddy. It's effort-free. As long as you're attracted enough that sex is a possibility and you feel safe, that's all that matters. Sex, done properly, makes you feel wonderfully accepted.

It's different from love. Maybe in the upper classes it's called a fling, but down here where I live it's a pressure release, and no love or imitation Hollywood romance or delusions of long-term commitment are required. It's not like I fuck everyone within arm's reach, but I don't expect to fall in love with everyone I've ever been infatuated with either. It's just nice to be in a pleasant spot for a while, that's all.

The coping that I and many of my friends do via medication isn't just about emotional relief. For me at least, it's just as much about physical pain management. I've stopped paying attention to how much ibuprofen I take in a day. More than I should, certainly. A reckless amount, even. I'm a pill popper, just not the narcotic sort. I start my day with ibuprofen and cold medicine, because I get sinus headaches from pretty much every part of nature and my jaw is always killing me. B12 for energy, vitamin C as a prophylactic measure. The ibuprofen starts to wear off in a couple hours, so I take some more. Repeat as necessary. Add in a pot of coffee and maybe a guilt-ridden switch to naproxen in the afternoon for pain management, plus whatever nicotine I get in there. And if I absolutely have to sleep well, I wind up taking something that says "p.m." on it, whatever that might be. If the pain is bad, as it often is for people with serious back injuries and dental problems like mine, alcohol or some kind of narcotics might be taken too. That, friends, is what pain management looks like outside the health care system.

Miraculously, I'm not dead yet, and as far as I know, my liver hasn't started to fail. My husband comes from healthy stock, the sort of people who maybe keep a bottle of aspirin around for emergencies. He was horrified at my intake, to the point that he once asked me to try not to take anything for a while to see if it would reset things for me. After a couple days I wound up in bed trying not to breathe too much because moving made the headache worse, and he's never mentioned it since.

I know that any actual cure of my chronic pain would have to at least partly involve lifestyle changes that simply haven't ever been logistically possible. Any kid who watches *Sesame Street* can tell you that it's important to sleep well, drink lots of water, and eat a balanced diet. And I can guarantee you that I can drink lots of water. The other two are trickier, if not mostly impossible.

A balanced diet is one more detail to throw at me, and for years my diet consisted of whatever food at work had become expired for service most recently—sometimes beef, sometimes chicken. And when I got home, I ate dinner only when I was absolutely starving. I ate food that I was craving, because it made me feel better. Healthy food, sad to say, just doesn't work as well as a pan of brownies when it comes to soothing yourself.

I've got way bigger problems than a spinach salad can solve.

A human body doesn't care if acute stress is caused by almost getting your electricity shut off or by a looming deadline on a million-dollar contract. The reason that poor people wind up coping in ways that seem pointlessly self-destructive is that all the constructive stuff costs money. I can't afford to join a gym. I can't just pay a shrink to listen to me vent. I can't go shopping or find an acupuncturist or a good masseuse or whatever else it is that the people above me do to cope. I can't pay someone to make my back relax when I have strained it, and we don't get to take it easy when it happens if we want to keep our hours at work.

Our bodies are no longer our temples. We can't afford for them to be. I have agreed, more than once, to let people have parts of my body for money. I have observed, lying on a bed to sell my plasma for twenty bucks, that it's the modern-day opium den—people languid on medical tables instead of couches, staring at the closest TV or watching in fascination as their own blood is separated in the machine.

But I have only so many body parts I can spare. Only so much blood.

There are millions of us who have had enough of this.

We have waited. We have been patient. We have coped. And we've survived, which we'll continue to do. Humans are amazingly resilient.

The question is, how can the rest of the country live knowing that so many of us have to live like this?

6

This Part Is About Sex

'm writing a chapter about sex, so I'm trying to remember the names of everyone I've slept with. I don't think it's possible; sobriety hasn't always been involved. I never bought the idea that sex is actually immoral. God made me human, so I tend to think he doesn't expect me to act like an angel, if in fact angels don't mess around. And I really don't understand why rubbing genitals with someone is immoral. With all the evil in the world, we're really going to judge people who make each other feel good?

Being poor is isolating. You're constantly being rude to friends and family because you never have time to talk, never have time to hang out. Never have the money to do anything, not even to reciprocate a birthday present. You don't ever have anything new happening—no news to share unless you're getting married or having a baby. You lose the most interesting parts of yourself to the demands of survival. I got so boring when I was at my worst that even *I* didn't want to hang out with myself. Why on earth would I invite anyone I liked to come over and stare at walls with me?

For me, sex has been a logical fix for that problem. It doesn't require conversation, no personality necessary. Just some skill and willingness and a partner with the same two things. It's catharsis without any baggage or investment. Sex is kind of magic that way; if you tell a woman she is beautiful, and you do it when you are as unguarded as you can possibly be, she will believe you, and it will stick with her. If you tell a man he is wanted, and you do it when you are making that very clear, he will remember your words longer than you do. You can fix people a little bit, plus there are orgasms and cuddling. I couldn't design better therapy.

Sex is fun. It's fun for rich people, it's fun for poor people. But there are two possible reasons for having sex that I think tend to be way more important to poor people than to rich people: 1) The chemical rush of sex is a great way to forget about your problems for a little while, and 2) sex is completely free.

Let's talk about the endorphin rush first. It's not just the thrill of an orgasm that I'm talking about. It's the physical comfort and feeling of a little pleasure in your body. Few things are more isolating than financial desperation. Sure I have my friends to talk to, but while we commiserate about the practical—the unpaid bills or the car troubles—we rarely talk about our feelings. We shy away from them. And when I come home from a long day at work, it's a guarantee that my husband has had just as sucky a day. If we want physical comfort and a loosening of the back muscles, it's only going to happen while we're having sex.

Given that the reason that I'm often in need of relaxation has to do with the lack of money, it's an added bonus that sex is also free. Entertainment costs. Movies, bowling, whatever you can think of that nice folks do on dates that don't involve sex—that's all a luxury. When you have nothing in your wallet and nothing else to do, sex is really good for killing time. I've spent more than one afternoon in bed because it was the only entertaining option I had. Given the choice between a) sex minus boredom, and b) celibacy plus boredom, I think we all know which one is preferable.

Wealthier people don't seem to understand it when some poor person pairs up with some other poor person who maybe isn't so perfect. Maybe doesn't have the greatest teeth, or the most steady employment, or the best attitude about the world. They seem to think that for every Julia

Roberts, there's a Richard Gere just waiting to catapult her into respectability. It's only among the wealthy that most people could potentially model for clothing catalogs. Marry up as a life strategy—sure! In real life, Julia would have married a recently laid-off cab driver.

We choose from what's available, after all. It's not like laureates and models are thick on the ground, and Richard Gere isn't going to show up to whisk me out of the strip club anytime soon. So I wind up with people who are as flawed as I am; people who work where I do and shop where I do and socialize where I do. It doesn't lend itself to meeting a millionaire and running off to a happily-ever-after in the Hamptons, or even the suburbs.

That doesn't mean we're indiscriminate. We do not simply drop trou and rut like animals upon spotting another human that we might be able to fuck. We have sex for the same reasons rich people do—we are in love, we liked someone's smile, someone made us laugh. Sometimes they're cute and there's a spark.

Of course the kind of cliché downward spiral about poor women is that once things get really bad, they have nothing left to sell but their bodies. That's probably the worst thing most rich people can imagine a poor person having to sink to. Well, that and starving to death. But don't we all trade sex for something? Even rich people do that—just ask one of those women you see with a big fat diamond on her finger and a boring and unattractive husband to go with it.

Living rent-free is a pretty good incentive for adding a sexual element to an existing friendship. More than once, someone has offered me a place to live when I needed one, and then kind of let me know we'd be having sex. It wasn't a power imbalance; it was just an understanding that, value for value, this was the deal. If I didn't like it, I could leave and no harm done. I could probably still have crashed for a day or two, just not long-term. It's sex as currency. Cutting the bills by moving in with someone you've only just started dating is less sexual than it is practical. If you have found someone who you get along with, who you enjoy the company of, and it's likely to last at least a few months, it just makes sense to move in together. There is no shame in it, and nor should there be.

I've been in less comfortable sorts of sex-as-barter scenarios at work, but I've never had to accept them. I could always quit or get fired. I was young when the offers were made and didn't have kids to feed or extended family counting on me. I was lucky; it never worked on me because I had other options.

That said, the situation isn't always as gross as that. Sex, as a commodity, isn't traded so explicitly and openly as "here is cash, now please fuck me" in all cases. Sometimes, it's a quid pro quo. Sometimes it's even between friends. I don't see a problem with that; it's a human need, and filling it thus has economic value. Related: If you want to have some fun, ask a free-market religious conservative whether you should restrict prostitution, given that there's a clear market demand for it.

And look, you can't blame people for leading with their assets. My occasional forays into the sex industry have convinced me that breasts really are magic. I got bigger tips as a bartender in a strip club when I wore a corset. We all exploit our advantages. There's something about a corset that turns an otherwise reasonable bar patron into something resembling a monkey. A very well-tipping monkey, to be fair.

The act of putting on a corset is enough to negate any dental problems, weight issues, or personality flaws. Guys would just see that three inches where a very specific kind of fat folds together and boom—instant idiots.

The girls who actually took their bras off made the real money, relatively speaking—it was more than I made but still not enough. If there was cash within five feet of a topless woman, it was often hers for the asking. The only reason I never did it myself is that while my breasts are big, they're also kind of wonky. And also I can't dance. And I would not be able to keep my temper through what I saw those girls deal with. So I kept to my spot behind the bar. Guys actually thought I'd be impressed when they told me that they liked me best out of all the women at the club because real honest women wouldn't strip, that it was beneath them to like a stripper. Amazing. Some guys will moralize at you *while they're getting a lap dance*. These guys were conflicted about their own sexual moral systems and they blamed us for it, which led to insanely entertaining scenes of dancer rage. You'd see a girl storming out of the lap dance area and a guy leaving just as mad. And she'd tell you that he'd been rude, demanded some seriously inappropriate, um, dance moves, and then told her she was going to hell. It didn't happen often, but it was gold every single time.

It's ridiculous to suggest that poor people should behave more appropriately about sexual matters than anyone else does. I am fairly certain I could walk into any swanky bar and find well-off people who are hoping for a night's fling. I can say with near certainty that most high-end sex clubs cater to wealthy patrons.

I like to remind people that everyone's parents fucked. Sex isn't dirty, isn't abnormal, shouldn't be a source of shame. Sadly, we as a society are a bit more conflicted about it than that. And for some reason, we moralize more at the poor about sex than we do at the population in general.

Living in low-income neighborhoods, I've seen sexual

health campaigns aimed at slut-shaming us into celibacy. They talk about things like self-esteem and value and all the usual abstinence arguments. They assume that our bodies are a gift that we should bestow selectively on others, rather than the one thing that can never be anything but our own. Even if we do share it, it is ours irrevocably.

These are the bodies that hold the brains we're supposed to shut off all day at work, the same bodies that aren't important enough to heal. These are the bodies that come with the genitalia that we should be so protective of? I really don't understand the logic.

You can't tell us that our brains and labor and emotions are worth next to nothing and then expect us to get all full of intrinsic worth when it comes to our genitals. Either we're cheap or we're not.

Make up your fucking mind.

7

We Do Not
Have Babies for
Welfare Money

I never expected to be a parent. I've got wonky hormones, and pregnancy was supposed to be a non-option for me; I was as surprised as anyone when I wound up getting pregnant. But once my husband and I had our oldest daughter, we decided we wanted a second child. Our kid needed a playmate, needed to learn to share, needed someone to join forces with against us. My husband's brother is only a few years younger than he is, and I'm forever hearing happy-childhood-with-Andy stories. As an only child, I have favorite childhood memories of times when I was utterly alone, sitting in a tree with a book. So Tom and I decided that for our child, we preferred the former.

So I never understand it when people want to know why

poor people have kids. I don't think having kids is a money question—why does anyone have a second child, or a third? Because their family feels unfinished. We have two children now, and we're done. We feel done. But we didn't feel that way before our youngest came along. That's why we had a second child. Why do rich people have kids? Do they sit around looking at their bank statements and decide it's a good time to procreate? So yeah, poor people get to have kids too. Deal with it.

But what about all those unplanned pregnancies that you're tut-tutting over? Let's talk about those first, and the whole subject of birth control. Then we'll go on to discuss what we do with our babies once we have them.

I mentioned that I thought kids weren't exactly likely for me and my husband. A lot of people in my situation would have taken their chances and skipped birth control altogether. But I had a firm belief, instilled in me by my girl heroes from the 1990s, that I should simply be on birth control on principle. Just in case. It was a feminist act, somehow. And I fucking hated it.

The pills made my moods uncontrollable. My periods came nice and regularly, but they were suddenly insane-flood level instead of anything manageable. I'd switch brands or types of birth control, only to discover some fresh hell.

Did you know that if you forget one crucial pill, just one day, you can wind up pregnant anyway? As it turns out, the odds of medicine working are much lower if you don't actually take it. I'm a forgetful person, to put it very nicely. The Pill and I didn't get along well.

Since I was with one person who had been tested since he'd been with anyone, and as I was in the same situation, I just sort of stopped bothering at all. Call it magical thinking, or trusting vague assurances from doctors, but I really didn't think I'd wind up pregnant, because I have never had normal lady parts. I also think I'd have been more vigilant if we didn't have some notions about having kids in the future. I thought maybe we'd adopt some foster kids, actually. We both came from families in which you married and then had kids, and that was likely what we'd do. We were having a lot of fun as a couple and weren't in any hurry to get to the next step, but in skipping birth control, we weren't actually risking more than bringing on a planned future.

So that's how I ended up pregnant without meaning to. Did that happen because I'm poor? Maybe. If I'd had the luxury of having a regular gynecologist who made it her mission to find a reliable form of birth control for me that didn't mess me up mentally and physically, then I almost certainly wouldn't have gotten pregnant when I did. And that's the thing about gynecology in this country—we seem to care about women's bodies only once they are pregnant.

Just like every other sector of health care, access to family-planning services is heavily dependent on income. But a good portion of the unplanned pregnancies I've seen in my circles weren't the result of an active lack of concern for the outcome or even access to contraception. Rather, the condom broke, the pills didn't work, someone miscounted. And then there are people like me who just thought they'd never get pregnant. That all happens to plenty of rich people too. Likewise those cases where the heat of the moment really just sort of blew their brains away for a minute and no birth control got used at all—I don't think that's really something you can say belongs to any one group of people.

I've got zero trouble walking into a Planned Parenthood clinic. I cannot say the same for a lot of women I know. There's a stigma attached to walking into a place that a lot of demagogues associate with abortions. I actually enjoyed my brush with the protesters; they kept telling me, "You don't have to do this" and "You have options." Since I was arriving at the clinic for my first ultrasound to make sure that the baby was healthy, I had a ball pretending to be outraged that they obviously wanted me to abort my baby. You know how sometimes you leave and you figure they'll get it in about five minutes, and you have won utterly? I totally got to do that with the protesters.

I've actually led a bit of a charmed life when it comes to family planning, at least compared with most poor women. That's because I don't give a fuck whether people think I'm a bit of a whore and I've generally lived near enough to cities that clinics aren't too far away. I've usually had a car and enough cash to spare. But man, that does not mean it's easy. First, the fees are unpredictable. I've paid ten bucks for a month of pills, and I've paid fifty. It depends on the funding of the clinic you visit.

And that's just the pills; you have to take off work, have a car that'll make the trip, and pay for gas to get there. In rural areas, it might be a few hours to the closest clinic. Of course, most people have a doctor in their hometown. But they might not have a low-income clinic, and even if they do, it might not do birth control. Some women don't want to get birth control locally, because we've actually been pretty successful at slut-shaming Pill users, as though there's no use for them beyond their contraceptive value. Lots of women would be ashamed to be discovered as medicated harlots.

I know a woman who has been married for five years. She and her husband are in college, hoping to start a family—just maybe in a few years instead of now. She will not visit a Planned Parenthood in Utah or ask for the Pill from her gynecologist, because she is terrified that someone will find out. And that's in Utah, where the dominant religion is all for married people using birth control. I can't imagine what it's like someplace where whore pills and birth control are synonymous.

Look, it's not like condoms are superexpensive. But they're not free, and we don't run across those bowls that you see on college campuses. And God help you if you're poor and allergic to latex. Then you just don't get to have sex.

Okay, so for whatever reason—whether you wanted kids or your birth control didn't work—congratulations, you're pregnant! Now what?

Here's a big secret from a poor person: Having a baby is expensive only if you want it to be. Let's go back to the rich-people-looking-at-the-bank-statement thing: A lot of rich people look for a new house or a new apartment before they even get pregnant. Because, the thinking goes, they must have a nursery, or they must have a second or third or fourth bedroom. God forbid kids should share a room. But kids don't care. Kids know what they know. Babies are happy in a drawer in their parents' bedroom, and if kids are used to sleeping in the same room with their brother or sister, then they are happy with the company. Sure they'll fight over space at some point, but I don't care how big your house is—your kids will fight over space. So let's just dismiss the whole idea that kids require a big real estate investment.

The idea of privacy among nuclear family members is actually pretty new. Parents used to share a bed with their kids—*and still expand their families somehow*. If people could manage to perpetuate the species with their toddlers thrashing around in the same space, well, I'm not going to bitch about having to share space too much.

Now let's get down to the real basics of what kids need. Sure, you can buy disposable diapers or spend forty bucks a pop on bespoke organic cotton for Junior to poop on. Or you can tear up old T-shirts. Babies don't really even care whether their butts are covered; we do that to avoid the cleaning up that would be needed otherwise. It's quite satisfying to buy thrift store T-shirts with logos of things you hate for a quarter a pop and tear them up so your baby can do her worst.

What I think people are talking about when they say that kids are expensive is either stuff that's so unattainable that we'd never have kids at all if we waited for it to come along, or stuff that's entirely unnecessary. When I got pregnant, I started reading up on the latest in parenting, which I'd really not been paying attention to at all. And I was mostly pretty appalled. There are whole articles in women's magazines about how to politely turn down hand-me-downs, like this is a major problem for some people. The idea of turning down hand-me-downs is so crazy to me that I don't even know where to start. Your kid will be able to use this stuff for only a few months. And kids absolutely massacre clothes. My youngest can be sitting in the middle of the living room with nothing in her reach, and within five minutes her clothes can pick up a stain from something that I'm not even sure is in the same room with her. For what possible reason, short of family photos or weddings, would you pay retail for something you can get free or secondhand?

Until your kid is old enough to start begging for toys (and this is one of the reasons why I don't have cable: no toy commercials, no begging), the only truly essential expenses you have to incur are for food and medical care.

I've talked about what it's like to be impoverished and pregnant, but the bare fact remains that I wound up pregnant and *then* hit full impoverishment. I had to figure out how I'd make it work. What I figured was this: Kids can eat pretty much everything adults can, and they don't eat nearly as much until they hit puberty. And thank God, WIC would cover formula until we were back on our feet.

I'm not being dismissive of hunger. I have known hungry children. The ones I've met have uniformly come from families that were overextended, that had cousins and close family friends crashing in their living rooms, or that had some medical emergency or long-term unemployment. There was always an actual external reason for their hunger. I've never met a parent that simply didn't bother to feed their kid. (I've no doubt they exist, but I've never met one—I think they're probably about as common as serial killers and receive as much publicity too.) The key is that it wasn't the having of the kids that was the backbreaking straw for these families.

Children, themselves, do not actually require much. Two families living on one poor person's income, though, or one family on no income, is impossible no matter how little they need. It's ridiculous to make the argument that people should be able to predict every possible downturn in their lives in advance. Poor people are not uniquely psychic. Just like rich people don't think, wow, maybe we shouldn't have kids because we might have an acrimonious custody battle someday, poor people don't decide not to have kids because they think, wow, maybe Aunt Jane will lose her job and have to come live with us with all her kids. And I'm using the extended-family example, but it could be any disaster—illness, whatever. The point is that people don't plan their lives around certain disaster. People who do are called paranoid.

And there are resources for families so their kids don't go hungry, ideally. On a daily level, there's WIC for formula, and once babies have outgrown that, they're old enough to eat whatever you're eating. I've heard critiques of that too— that you shouldn't have kids if you're not going to feed them a healthy diet (which apparently consists of organic kale and quinoa, because it's not like poor kids have never seen bananas or apples). What we eat is generally fine for our kids, at least according to the food safety people. And people do tend to buy healthier food when they have kids in the house, from what I've seen. I know we do. My kids eat a lot of fruit. A lot. My three-year-old is obsessed with all the different kinds of fruit in the world; we go to grocery stores and she picks it out and we call it a good choice. She eats chicken nuggets and fries, sure, but not constantly. Mostly, she eats a bit of my sandwich or her dad's noodles or whatever it is we're making.

I can promise you that I did not buy much fruit before the kids came along. I rarely bought anything perishable outside of the requisite coffee creamer and milk. So yes, believe it or not, poor people do sometimes make smart decisions just for their children's sake.

Yet hunger is still a real thing. I've been there. I didn't qualify for food stamps at one point because on paper we were said to be getting a living stipend from the VA. I know this sounds crazy, but hear me out and maybe (if you don't already) you will finally understand why being poor and qualifying for benefits is not the same as being poor and actually getting benefits. I've briefly mentioned before that we didn't get a stipend from the VA that we'd been promised. So here's what happened: Basically, we were awarded a certain amount of money through the GI Bill. Because of a paperwork error on the part of the university, the VA never actually mailed us the living stipend I've mentioned. And they knew this, and acknowledged this, as did the folks at SNAP to whom we applied for food stamps. However, simply because the government *said* that we should be getting $1,200, we were disqualified from receiving food stamps. Despite the fact that everyone involved agreed that the money was theoretical and that we didn't actually have it. We eventually got it cleared up, but it was one more thing to deal with.

When I think about that, I hope that the people who want to make sure that they weren't feeding a single person who isn't abject are happy. I know I certainly felt better about the state of the country watching my husband being thanked for his service by the people telling him that they'd be rejecting him for food aid. So, dear voters and policymakers who are very, very afraid that a poor person might illicitly have a decent steak for their birthday: Thanks for the months of ramen.

I have the solution to hungry children in America. Nobody wants to do it, but here goes: Fucking feed people. Cancel the programs where we pay farmers not to farm, and grow food. Buy it from them and use it in schools. Create real jobs. Fund SNAP. Stop calling it welfare and start calling it something that describes what it is: a subsidy like any other so that the people actually moving this huge wheel of capitalism can live decent, maybe basic but still pleasant lives. Hunger: solved.

Now let's talk about health care, which obviously kids need. There's a thing called the Children's Health Insurance Program. Its income standards aren't as stringent as Medicaid's. Most kids who need it qualify. It's not the same as being able to take your kid to the doctor for every sniffle, but if they have a serious fall or a scary spike in temperature, you can call a nurse. We can also take them to the ER, which is where the pediatrician tells you to go if it's an acute situation anyway. In general, poor parents know what to do for minor maladies, and we know our kids will be taken care of if it's catastrophic and we're not working at a place that offers insurance.

But just because poor people can't afford to be hysterical about our kids' health doesn't mean we're blasé. I was sitting on a park bench one time when my daughter came screaming over to demand that I kiss her knee better. She'd scraped it somehow—it looked worse than it was.

So I kissed it and sent her back to play. Another mom, clearly in a different tax bracket, turned to me to ask whether I needed to borrow her antiseptic; I said we were fine. And then she told me how she'd really like to be able to be so nonchalant about her baby being hurt. I wasn't sure whether she was trying to be cutting or really meant it; either way, my brain started demanding I cross the vast gulf between "not making a big fuss over a skinned knee" and "nonchalant about my child being hurt." They're different things. Way different things. So, rich lady who thinks I'm nonchalant? Mind your own business. And maybe sometimes, when your little princess skins her knee, send her back out to play instead of acting as though she'd just lost a limb.

It's good for them, you know.

Once we move past all the daily subsistence-level stuff that we really need to worry about, the question seems to change from "Why do you have kids you can't afford to take care of?" to "Why don't you take care of your kids in the exact manner of which I approve?"

Take college, for example. Many rich people look at poor people and think it's disgusting that we can't afford to give our kids a good education. Or maybe they think we deserve it for being poor. Either way, I know they think that our kids' educations are suffering because of our class status. As if we haven't thought about this or don't have a plan. Well, newsflash, we do. My husband and I will do what our parents did. We'll make sure our kids are curious, well-read people. We'll make sure they get good grades. We'll make them study. And when it comes time, we'll see what sorts of scholarships and grants they qualify for and then probably take out loans for the rest. I guess I don't really see how my plan is that much different from a wealthier person's until you hit the "we'll just pay for it" level. Is it really the end of the world to go to a state school?

I think there's also a judgment leveled at poor parents that we give our kids a terrible quality of life, as if our children are deeply conscious of their poverty on a daily basis. And certainly, there are a lot of people who've been plunged into circumstances so bad that they can't keep their kids ignorant of it. But lots of people are just struggling to get by, and they're doing so without irreparably harming their children. Maybe things aren't picture-perfect all the time, but I don't see the value in that anyway. I promise that if, like I did, you paint rainbows on your kids' walls, it'll be a decade or so before they realize that it's crooked and definitely not a professional job. You might notice. I notice. My kids? They think it's a pretty fucking cool rainbow.

That's what I love about kids—everything is magic for them. If you tell them the world is awesome, and you make sure awesome things sometimes happen, they will totally go with you on that one. Awesome, to a kid, is a rainbow wall or a tickle fight or a hiding place in the closet. They don't realize that collecting every My Little Pony is awesome un-less you tell them it is. Class, the relative having of things—that stuff doesn't come up until later. Until we put it there. Kids will not notice worn spots in their clothes until they are socialized to. They simply don't get social constructs, class included. We raise our children to believe whatever we decide they should. And like most poor people, I'll raise my kids to be resourceful and aware. At some point, I will dis-cuss class with them, just like every parent will discuss the real world with their children.

The point is that my kids are loved and they know it. I've heard a lot of young women give that reason for having their babies, actually: love. I come from a culture where the girls marry young and the families are big. It's just how we roll in Utah. I've actually seen people have numbered jerseys made for their kids when they made a full team's worth. That is considered cute where I come from.

I've heard it said that poor people have kids because they want someone to love them unconditionally. But I think it's more nuanced than that. I think that the stereotypical teen-age wannabe mom who gives that reason wants someone she can safely love, someone who is predictable and steady and will stick around no matter what. And yes, it's sad for a young girl to feel that way. That said, I can understand it. In Utah, where we often marry young and have babies young, young women might think, "I may as well get started being an adult and having a family." Is it the wisest course? No. But it's not crazy. It's not even unrealistic. It's not like these girls have brilliant futures in the Ivy League that they're passing up to have babies; those are typically reserved for the children of brilliant Ivy Leaguers. They are deciding to have their toddlers while they themselves are young and have the energy. And plenty of people, no matter where they are from, simply have love to give.

What really riles me is this idea that poor people are somehow inherently more selfish when we have children. There are plenty of rich people who have kids for exactly the same reasons I just described—because they want someone who will love them unconditionally, and with whom they can share that kind of all-encompassing love. But somehow, because they have money, rich people are entitled to feel that way without being derided. Let's not kid ourselves, though, that it's any less selfish or self-centered.

What, after all, is Baby Gap and its ilk appealing to, if not parents who enjoy dressing up their kids as little mini-mes? Trust me, no infant has a serious desire to wear a cable-knit V-neck sweater with a collared shirt underneath, no matter how adorable they look. Preschool prep classes? Not meant for the kid's self-esteem. So the problem of child-bearing as an extension of your own personal brand sort of transcends social class.

———

Truth time: We do not breed for sweet, sweet government cheese.

I understand that some people will say, "But you just said that everything was cool because of welfare!" I can see how one might come to that objection if you're only working on what you have read in this book so far. But trusting that you will always at least be able to feed your family, even if it is at food banks and with SNAP, is a whole different ball game from actively deciding to have a child specifically for the money.

Okay, quick lesson time. Welfare isn't a thing. That is to say, welfare is a lot of things as opposed to one thing. And each of these things has different requirements. It's not hard to qualify for some things, relatively speaking. If you're starving, you can pretty much count on qualifying for SNAP or food bank services. Now, access to those things can be sketchy, but that's a different point. The point here is that food benefits can be spent only on food; the benefit card blocks anything that isn't approved. Cash benefits, the ATM-withdrawal kind of welfare—money that you can use on rent, gas, the water bill, clothing—are actually damn near impossible to qualify for. And to get them, you've got to jump through a lot of extra hoops. Cash benefits are the ones tied to work or looking for work or training for work or working for the state.

If you are desperate enough to be breeding for cash benefits, you are for all practical purposes having kids in order to be poor enough for the government to give you a full-time job. See, the reason everyone says that you get more money for having kids is that your benefits are determined by both your income and household size. So, to make it an income stream, you have to decrease your non-benefit income and/or increase your household size sufficiently. That, I think, is probably pretty rare. And if you think about it for a few seconds, I think you will see how ridiculous the whole idea of it is. It would be like breaking your leg so you can go to the hospital because they'll feed you while you're there.

I definitely have told that joke once or twice—that I was having kids for the sweet, sweet government cheese—but hello? I *meant* it as a joke. Granted, I do think there are many stupid people out there. There are stupid rich people and there are stupid poor people. The stupid rich people think that welfare queens are breeding like rabbits. And sure, there are probably a few people out there who did not realize even after Kid One that kids are a giant pain in the ass. Maybe a few of those idiots thought they'd make an easy paycheck by having another kid. But I'd argue that there are a lot fewer of these poor idiots than those rich idiots think there are. And by a "lot fewer," I mean a statistically insignificant number of poor people are doing this. Can I prove this? No. But nor can I prove that people aren't breaking their legs just to get some lunch.

I'm not even certain how people think it's possible that someone would have kids for welfare benefits. Do these people not have kids of their own? Did they manage to sleep through the colic somehow, or did they simply block it out? I mean, if you're going to pay me in multiple tens of thousands of dollars a year to have a kid, okay, maybe it's worth thinking about. But a few thousand dollars extra, best-case scenario, and that's my entire income and I'll still be living this desperate life? Yeah, no, I'll pass on that deal.

To accept the idea that someone would have babies just for the money, you have to assume that they see their children as stock rather than as kids. The more temperate assumption that follows is that poor people neglect their kids. But what wealthier people view as neglect is pretty shallow stuff and to me is just a matter of taste. My kids have dirty faces sometimes. Unless we're going somewhere or expecting someone, my husband and I really don't bother making sure they're spotless. It's a losing battle with toddlers. Our kids are both fascinated with baths, so they're always pretty clean overall, but their faces and hands are a different story. Most people I know are the same way; we just don't have the time or energy to chase little kids down and demand that they keep their hands clean. They're little, they're *supposed* to ignore the lawn in favor of the mud puddles.

That said, I'd be horrified if they left the house like that. I think most people are that way in secret, inclined to be a bit lax at home. It doesn't speak to your actual parenting skills, I think, although the state of your children's faces when nobody's watching is a clear indicator of whether or not you lean toward OCD.

I'm not saying that there are no standards, just that maybe some of them could use some loosening. And of course there's a line you're just not supposed to cross. There's being a bit lax, and then there's being legitimately a kind of awful parent. Don't worry, poor people disapprove of those people in Walmart screaming empty threats at their kids at top volume too.

But I think it's a little misguided when wealthier people turn up their noses at the parenting style of poor people who don't necessarily treat their children like precious china that would break if looked at sideways. I'm not preparing our kids for a gentle world, full of interesting and stimulating experiences. I'm getting them ready to keep their damn mouths shut while some idiot tells them what to do. I'm preparing them to keep a sense of self when they can't define themselves by their work because the likeliest scenario is that (unlike doctors and lawyers and bankers) they will not want to. I'm getting them ready to scrap and hustle and pursue happiness despite the struggle.

I think a lot of what people see as bad parenting is simply that our kids have different expectations. It wouldn't make any sense to take wealthy kids and prepare their brains for drudge work. And it doesn't make much sense to take poor kids and prepare them to seek fulfillment from work. That's not how it goes for us. If they find it, that's fantastic. But odds are, they will work just as many zombie jobs as they will good ones.

I'll teach my kids to be curious, to learn stuff for themselves because learning is kind of awesome for its own sake, to find what interests them and get obsessive about it. But learning and thinking is only a hobby for the working class, and I think it's best they're prepared. You never know what their lives will be. The happiest people are the ones who can simply block out the worst of it.

When I gave birth to my oldest daughter, I was visited more than once in the hospital by authorities because I'd had no prenatal care. They asked invasive are-you-an-idiot questions. All the questions seemed designed to make me look like an unfit parent: One of them was "Do you have a job?" My answer was "Not at the moment." (True—I'd quit work just before giving birth and didn't intend to look for more work for another two weeks.) Another was "Do you have a permanent home?" My answer to that was also no. (This was during the time when our apartment was flooded and we were fighting with our landlord about our housing.) I was asked my education level (college dropout), and I was even asked if anyone in my home had a diagnosed mental disorder. Yep. After all this, I was pretty convinced they weren't going to let me take my daughter home. Luckily, I dodged that bullet. She was healthy enough, and it's not like I was the first uninsured woman to get pregnant in a century or anything.

A neighbor of mine was investigated because she was at work *too much*. And they asked her the same sorts of questions, meant to find fault: How many hours are you gone? Have you considered cutting back? She said that they spoke a lot about marriage during her sessions, like making her boyfriend a permanent fixture was some kind of panacea. (The dude was useless, and as far as I could tell, he was her one indulgence.) The whole time these authorities were shaming her for working so much, she was thinking about nannies. See, if she'd been wealthy enough to hire a nanny, it wouldn't matter how much she was gone. She was talking to the authorities only because she didn't get paid enough.

I knew a guy, a single dad, who had two girls. One in particular decided to be a hell-raiser; she started fights at school, stole beer from the fridge and gave it to her friends (of course on school property), and generally made herself a giant pain in his ass. I don't think anyone really blamed the girl; being motherless at thirteen can't be easy, and her mom had died not too long previously. It was the sort of situation that, I imagine, wealthy kids get some extra consideration, maybe some therapy for. Instead, they sent the dad to jail for contributing to the delinquency of a minor. Needless to say, he lost his kids. He's been spending every penny he's got ever since, trying to regain custody.

Are these irresponsible parents who deserve to have their kids taken away—or to have even the threat of that held over their heads? No. They're just poor people who love their kids and are doing the best that they can for them with limited resources. So let's stop saying that poor people are irresponsible parents and start admitting that society doesn't seem to believe that if you are poor you are entitled to be a parent at all.

Given how easy it is to lose our kids, it's no wonder that many poor people avoid any brushes with authority. We've learned how truly defenseless we are, so we just stay away. And what's the biggest authority in most children's lives? School.

My kids are still little, but I am not looking forward to dealing with a school once they hit that age. I'm afraid my kid's going to repeat something she heard at home between me and her dad. For example, our endless *South Park* references. What if someone hears her say something from the episode in which Cartman feeds a kid his own dead parents to make up for a pubic hair scam and assumes that we're teaching our kid about the joys of revenge via forced cannibalism? Is a woman from social services going to show up at my door and start asking questions about my salary and employment? Will it matter that she hasn't actually seen this happening, only heard us reference it in passing?

I've got it relatively easy here. I was well educated through much of my childhood. I don't have to feel awkward going to a parent-teacher meeting for my kid. I don't have to deal with a language barrier. I don't have to deal with getting the shaming that single parents so frequently come in for: Your child needs you home, you're not doing enough, you have to find more hours in the day or you're a bad parent.

When I was living in California, a Spanish-speaking neighbor asked me to read her a letter from her kids' school. The letter was full of impressive words. Words like "responsibility" and "consequences" and "requirements." She had been ducking the school for weeks because they'd required her son to participate in some fund-raising program and he owed the school money for not hitting his minimum sales. She didn't have it, so she stopped answering their calls. When she got this letter, which was a wordy "what we're up to" newsletter deal, she thought it was a collection notice. I tried to explain that he'd get to go to school regardless of a $20 debt, but I couldn't convince her. She simply didn't believe me. And the truth is, given how badly I've seen poor people treated by whatever system they're forced to deal with, I didn't really believe me either.

What it comes down to, then, is the idea that the *very same situations and behaviors* are treated completely differently depending on how nice your stuff is. Kid gets into a fight at school? If he's black and poor, he's going to jail. If he's rich and white, he's going to military school. Was your daughter busted with drugs? If she's poor, she's getting charged. If she's rich, she'll go to a nice rehab facility for however long propriety demands. The only reason it looks like our kids misbehave more is that we can't afford to cover up for them when they do.

During World War II, we had government-sponsored day care facilities. It was generally acknowledged that single-parent households, which the families left behind by the soldiers were, needed extra support. Maybe, and this is just a thought, we could do that again. Child-care crisis solved. Plus, it's another jobs program.

I'm not saying that poor kids have the same opportunities as rich kids. They don't. And that's bullshit. But that is not the same thing as saying that the poor are not capable of being decent, loving parents of decent people.

Besides. If we don't keep having kids, who do you think is going to work in tomorrow's restaurants? *Your* kids?

8

Poverty Is Fucking Expensive

I once lost a whole truck over a few hundred bucks. It had been towed, and when I called the company, they told me they'd need a few hundred dollars for the fee. I didn't have a few hundred dollars. So I told them when I got paid next and that I'd call back then.

It was a huge pain in the ass for those days. It was the rainy season, and I wound up walking to work, adding another six miles or so a day to my imaginary pedometer. It was my own fault that I'd been towed, really, and I spent more than a couple of hours hating myself. I finally made it to payday, and when I went to get the truck, they told me that I now owed over a thousand dollars, nearly triple my paycheck. They charged a few hundred dollars a day in storage fees. I explained that I didn't have that kind of money, couldn't even get it. They told me that I had some few months to get it together, including the storage fee for however long it took me to get it back, or that they'd simply sell it. They would, of course, give me any money above and beyond their fees if they recovered that much.

I was working two jobs at the time. Both were part-time. Neither paid a hundred bucks a day, much less two.

I wound up losing my jobs. So did my husband. We couldn't get from point A to point B quickly enough, and we showed up to work late, either soaked to the skin or sweating like pigs, one too many times. And with no work, we wound up losing our apartment.

It's amazing that the things which are absolute crises for me are simple annoyances for people with money. Anything can make you lose your apartment, because any unexpected problem that pops up, like they do, can set off that Rube Goldberg device.

One time I lost an apartment because my roommate got a horrible flu that we suspected was maybe something worse because it lingered forever—she missed work, and I couldn't cover her rent. Once it was because my car broke down and I missed work. Once it was because I got a week's unpaid leave when the company wanted to cut payroll for the rest of the month. Once my fridge broke and I couldn't get the landlord to fix it, so I just left. Same goes for the time that the gas bill wasn't paid in a utilities-included apartment for a week, resulting in frigid showers and no stove. That's why we move so much. Stuff like that happens.

Because our lives seem so unstable, poor people are often seen as being basically incompetent at managing their lives. That is, it's assumed that we're not unstable because we're poor, but rather that we're poor because we're unstable. So let's talk about just how fucking impossible it is to keep your life from spiraling out of control when you have no financial cushion whatsoever. And let's also talk about the ways in which money advice is geared only toward people who actually have money in the first place.

I once read a book for people in poverty, written by someone in the middle class, containing real-life tips for saving pennies and such. It's all fantastic advice: Buy in bulk, buy a lot when there's a sale, hand-wash everything you can, make sure you keep up on vehicle and indoor-filter maintenance.

Of course, very little of it was actually practicable. Bulk buying in general is cheaper, but you have to have a lot of money to spend on stuff you don't actually need yet. Hand-washing saves on the utilities, but nobody actually has time for that. If I could afford to replace stuff before it was worn out, vehicle maintenance wouldn't be much of an issue, but you really can't rinse the cheap filters again and again— quality costs money up front. In the long term, it makes way more sense to buy a good toaster. But if the good toaster is thirty bucks right now, and the crappiest toaster of them all is ten, it doesn't matter how many times I have to replace it. Ten bucks it is, because I don't have any extra tens.

It actually costs money to save money.

And it even costs more to get to your money if you're poor. One of the reasons that Walmart is so popular among the serving class is that it costs three bucks to cash your paycheck—flat fee. And they let you keep all of it but for that fee. Banks, on the other hand, are a giant pain in the ass. I loathe them, actually. Not fire-of-a-thousand-suns level, but I don't enjoy being in them. They seem to me to exist only to take your money. I've heard that wealthy people don't have to pay fees for everything, but if you're poor and don't have so much money to put in the bank, then you fall below their minimum balances and even accessing your money can cost you money.

Banks are useless to me. If you run low on cash, they take some more money just to punish you for not having enough money, and then they charge you $25 because, now that they've taken your money, you actually have negative money. That's nearly 10 percent of your *next* paycheck already. Besides which, banks are generally across town because they don't put banks in the places poor people live. They're always closed by the time you make it there from work, and the tellers always start being that kind of superior polite when they see your account balance.

I don't have a bank account for one reason: I am paranoid. I want my money, what I have of it, near me at all times. Otherwise, somebody might take it. I've had bank accounts just so that I could receive direct deposits from my employer. But since prepaid cards for payroll came out, I simply haven't needed a bank. They charge you $10 up front to set up the card and $5 a month in fees. The end.

I know that banks are where you go to get a loan, and that if you put your money in the bank and it stays there forever, you get good rates on things, but I don't get large loans and I don't have cash to just leave somewhere, so that doesn't really help me. And I can't get small loans there either.

That's why poor people pay insane interest rates. No matter what sort of credit rating you have, if your car's water pump goes out, you can't get a $300 loan from a bank. When something like that happens, some small emergency that I can't actually afford until the next paycheck, I've generally had three options: a payday loan, borrowing from friends, or doing without. My friends aren't always exactly flush themselves, leaving me with two choices: make it to work or not. When I've lived in the country or cities without good public transportation, making it to work has generally meant payday loans.

I'm kind of torn about payday lenders—the storefront small lenders that everyone's up in arms about. The way these places work is pretty simple: You give them some kind of collateral, like a postdated check if you have a checking account, or a car title. In the nicer ones, you don't need collateral, but you have to give them more paperwork about your income and a whole list of people you know. They call every one of them, and if all the references check, you get the loan.

Then you are allowed to borrow somewhere between $100 and $1,000 usually, and you pay an extortionate APR. Like, hundreds and hundreds of percentage points. But because the loan is so short, it's a relatively small amount of money in practice. If you can just pay it back with your next check and make it, then you're fine.

The reason people are up in arms, though, is that typically that's not the case. Most people can't take that full hit the next pay period either, so they roll over the loan. Then they wind up getting stuck and basically paying rent for the use of the money until they can pay it off. Worse, if anything happens before they do, then they have to take out another loan to cover *that*, and they can't do that at the same place. So then they owe two of these places money.

And payday lenders are brutal about getting it back. If any one of my employees was in default, we'd dread answering the phone. They'd call constantly. And they call for years. Meanwhile, clearly it's usury to charge 400 percent APR.

So I should be wholeheartedly against them, right? But the thing is, I'm not. Because they do serve a purpose that no one else does for poor people. I don't think in terms of annual APRs when I'm getting a payday loan. I think of it as a $15 poor tax. Every time we need to borrow $100 for a week, it costs $15. Are these places preying on the weak? Yep. Is it less moral than huge banks preying on the same demographic? Probably not, and those assholes have never bailed me out of a tight spot before. The payday places, evil empire though they are and all, actually do fill a niche where there's a real need. I've used them in the aforementioned water pump scenario and once when I got the flu and missed three days' work on a week I couldn't afford a short pay-check. Once it was because my husband's birthday was two days before payday and I'd put in extra shifts, so the expense was doable. I considered waiting until after, but his birthday was a day that we both had off, something nearly impossible to manage in an average week. We'd both requested it off months in advance, and I hadn't bothered to count ahead and remember which pay period to ask for extra hours. It was totally worth $15.

I figure that at some point it will occur to someone, somewhere, that the reason there are so many payday loan places is that there are so many people whose checks simply will not last a whole pay period unless everything goes perfectly, and that people who have things like perfect weeks aren't the sorts of people who've ever cashed a check at Walmart at three a.m. because they ran out of the napkins they'd been using as toilet paper for two days. Those people will find a less shitty way of doing business; perhaps someone can start a nonprofit bank that charges minimum fees or something. For now, we have our fees to pay.

I put furniture rental in the payday loan column because rental places are in the business of letting poor people have nice things for more than retail. The rental is simple; it's just making twelve easy payments of $99.99 for something that might actually cost closer to $1,000 if you paid it all at once. You are renting to own, so there's no risk; you just pay them when the bill's due, and when you're done, you own some furniture. In the meantime, you have some furniture, which is handier than the saving-up thing because sometimes you actually need a bed. Plus furniture rental places are pretty decent about you missing a week or two if you're having a rough patch, provided you generally pay on time and it doesn't happen too often. They get more interest that way.

Our economy seems to be run on credit, and it really doesn't serve poor people well. I get running credit checks on employees that will be working with cash or jewels or incredibly expensive bits of duck or something. But you can find job listings informing you that you'll need a credit check to be a receptionist or lawn guy. I guess maybe you could theoretically bribe an indebted receptionist for company secrets, but what's a gardener going to do? Not mow the lawn? I don't understand what credit—which is purportedly to see whether you're financially stable—has to do with whether you can mow grass. And I *really* don't get what being poor has to do with being a good driver, but I know that if you've got good credit, you get cheaper car insurance. This basically ensures that rich people pay less for car insurance than poor people do. Which I hope we all can agree is both ironic and tragic.

This is the part where people say, "But credit isn't *just* an indicator of finance! It's an indicator of trustworthiness and character!"—which would be fine if so many people of perfectly wonderful character weren't poor. Some of us are excited to do our very best every day. Lots of people who are lacking in resources are, you know, average people. Normal, with typical characters.

The real reason poor people have bad credit is that life is more expensive than we can tolerate. Again, see medical bills: not fucking likely we're going to have the money for those anytime soon. The vast majority of the poor people I know have terrible credit, and this affects every aspect of our lives. Whether or not you're currently doing okay, if you've got a poor credit score, you're going to have trouble finding anyone to rent to you. So poor people tend to be scraping the bottom of the barrel when they're looking for a new place to live—they're basically moving into the places that no one else wants.

It just adds insult to injury that for people who don't have enough money to buy something, landlords require that you cough up the equivalent of three months' rent—first, last, and security deposit—right at the outset. And that's just to get the keys to the place. Then you have to pay deposits on all the utilities to get them turned on. You might see a new tenant with no electricity for a couple of weeks and no gas for another pay period after that. I've done it. I just stayed with friends for the first few weeks I had the apartment. Then I moved in when the power went on. It's a last resort, when the schedules don't match up and you need to move your stuff before you can cover the power bill.

All this really rocked me when I got out into the big wide world, actually; you've got to come up with $1,000 or more as a security deposit just to move into a different shitty apartment. And this is for a $400-a-month studio—in addition to the first and last months' rent. And good luck getting that security deposit back when you move out. The landlord will argue that you put the cracks in the wall and that's it. I've lived in buildings where residents would actually warn new renters about it, because no one could recall a single security deposit ever being refunded. Sure, if you have the benefit of parents who will co-sign the lease for you, then you can possibly avoid having to pay such a high deposit. But I didn't have that option. Many of us don't.

There are housing voucher programs, of course. There's a subsidized housing program called Section 8, which seems to be pretty much the only game in town no matter where I've lived, excepting some religious charities. Basically, the government gives you a rent voucher if you qualify, and you get a list of approved apartments to pick from. I've sometimes wished I lived in Section 8 units, because the management company has to make sure that the doors and windows and all the appliances work properly in those apartments. I lived in a mixed building once, half Section 8 and half self-pay. Those of us paying cash found that we got less maintenance done on our apartments because the government wasn't picking up the tab for part of the rent and therefore wasn't insisting on regular inspections. The people who have the feds making sure their apartments are at least basically maintained live in . . . well, the places aren't falling apart. It's actually one of the things the government inspects for—visible cracks in the walls or ceilings.

The waiting list is typically long for subsidized housing. Eight years in DC, three in Houston. I've never seen one under two years. And I've never found it worth getting on the list, because I am unlikely to live in the same county and have a two-year-long bad spell. If your income changes while you're on the list, you're supposed to call and tell them. Then you're off the list. Unless you know for certain that you will not be doing any better for at least a couple of years, it's not even worth filling out the paperwork.

We can do better than this. We choose not to.

It is impossible to be good with money when you don't have any. Full stop. People tell me to save, not to buy luxuries like basic entertainment or communication or expensive food like hamburgers or pretty much any seafood according to Fox News (Dear *The Daily Show*: More of those segments, please), that those things are reserved for people better than me—read people with disposable income. And to the people who say that, I have only the wise words of Dick Cheney: Go fuck yourself.

If I'm saving my spare $5 a week, in the best-case scenario I will have saved $260 a year. For those of you who think in calendar quarters: $65 per quarter in savings. If you deny yourself even small luxuries, that's the fortune you'll amass. Of course you will never manage to actually save it; you'll get sick at least one day and miss work and dip into it for rent. Gas prices will spike and you'll need it to get to work. You'll get a tear in your work pants that you can't patch. Something, I guarantee you, will happen in three months.

When I have a few extra dollars to spend, I can't afford to think about next month—my present-day situation is generally too tight to allow me that luxury. I've got kids who are interested in their quality of life right now, not ten years from now. My whole family can be completely content for hundreds of hours for that money. Would some rich people think it was scandalous that a poor person would spend money on a game system? Probably, but that rich person can go to hell. Escape is the thing I value most, and it's a thing we'll sacrifice for.

When it comes to money, I think in value, not in sums. If I run a hundred dollars short, I can call in the loans and get my rent together, or just run up against the grace period for late payments. Or possibly I will be sort of fucked; it depends on whether or not I find a solution to the short-term problem. The only rational thing to do, really, is try to enjoy yourself as much as you can, if this is to be your life.

Here's the thing: We know the value of money. We work for ours. If we're at $10 an hour, we earn 83 cents, before taxes, every five minutes. We know exactly what a dollar's worth; it's counted in how many more times you have to duck and bend sideways out the drive-through window. Or how many floors you can vacuum, or how many boxes you can fill.

It's impossible to win, unless you are very lucky. For you to start to do better, something has to go right—and stay that way for long enough for you to get on your feet. I've done well in years that I had a job I didn't mind terribly and that paid me well enough to get into an apartment that met all the basic standards. I've done less well in years where I didn't have steady work. The trouble's been that my luck simply hasn't held out for long enough; it seems like just when I've caught up, something happens to set me back again. I've been fortunate enough that it's rarely compounded, and I've stayed at under sea level for short periods instead of long-term. But I've stared long-term in the face long enough to have accepted it as a real possibility. It's only an accident and a period of unemployment away.

It feels like I'm always climbing up the same hill, always trying to make it to neutral. And I don't have the stamina of Sisyphus to keep me going.

9

Being Poor Isn't a Crime—It Just Feels Like It

think that I might be a felon. My crime? Moving from Ohio to Utah. We were getting food stamps in Ohio, and I called the state to let them know to shut down our account. We applied for food stamps when we got to Utah and were approved. But it turns out Ohio didn't actually shut our account. They kept giving us money instead. Utah told us that we needed to call Ohio back, which we did. We were assured that the mistake was fixed. We called back Utah, who told us that we were still Ohio recipients. The state of Utah called Ohio. Three times. After that, our caseworker told us she didn't have time to deal with those people.

The thing is, it's no wonder Utah couldn't get through to Ohio—there's one welfare office for all of Hamilton County, which includes Cincinnati. One. For Cincinnati. That would be like having one Starbucks for all of Manhattan, or one tiny dog store for all of Los Angeles.

Now, it's illegal to use welfare benefits if you are not a resident of the state issuing them. So we found ourselves with a food stamp card that had an ever-increasing balance that we couldn't use. Every time we called, Ohio's worker would confirm that yes, there was a file in which they could see that we'd been asking them to stop giving us money for months. They'd apologize. None of them could figure out what the problem was. Each of them assured us that they'd fixed the problem.

We used the Utah benefits for a few months, until we got on our feet. And then we got the bill. As it turns out, even though Utah was perfectly aware that we couldn't help Ohio's clerical errors, and that we'd spent dozens of hours trying to get them to fix it, the law still holds us responsible for the duplication of benefits and calls it fraud. We were responsible for paying back the state.

Of course I called the state when we got the letter. Our caseworker apologized the entire time she was telling us how completely fucked we were. We'd only just gotten on our feet and we now owed the state more money than we made in a month. Oh, and while we were dealing with that hit, we'd be unable to get any additional help, because now that we were just on our feet, we didn't qualify for anything.

So it's no wonder that I don't have a lot of respect for authority or authoritative institutions. I'm so used to seeing people being punished for things they haven't done wrong, I'm pretty much always half sure I'm in violation of a law. And I'm not even being particularly paranoid in saying that—in a country where loitering is considered a crime, cops can pretty much arrest you at will. Refusing to tell cops anything they want to know is also criminally punishable should you run into a cop who's willing to stretch the meaning of "obstruction" or "impeding." You don't have to be robbing a bank to be a criminal. You just have to be poor and down on your luck and fall asleep on a park bench. I was recently on a college campus and saw at least three kids passed out on benches or at tables. I was tempted to call campus security to report the scourge of people resting. It turns out that whether sleeping on a public bench is a crime or not depends entirely on whether you have enough money to look like you have a place to sleep.

Another funny thing: It's incredibly easy to pick up a misdemeanor while actively trying not to get a DUI. If you walk home from the bar because you're drunk, or if you stay home in the first place but drink in your front yard, you are publicly intoxicated. Never mind that your front yard is where the afternoon and evening shade are and that you are very clearly just hanging out with your friends who are all of legal age, or that you misjudged and are wasted but can get home safely enough if you simply put one foot in front of the other down the correct roads. The fact that you left your car at the bar knowing that you shouldn't drive and you don't have cab fare will not be a mitigating factor. Your one solid bit of judgment that evening will potentially be punished severely.

People seem to be increasingly afraid of the poor—building gated communities and taking separate entrances—but it's not like criminal behavior as we think of it has suddenly skyrocketed. We've just made more shit illegal. And once you have a criminal conviction, best of motherfucking luck getting a job if unemployment is above zero. I've seen people get criminal records for stuff that you really wouldn't expect. You know that level of criminality where you just sort of shake your head, like toilet-papering a house or jay-walking? It's still criminal. I worked with a woman whose son, maybe thirteen or so, was in juvenile detention for rapping loudly outside after curfew. Now, I'm not saying it isn't annoying to have some kid outside being rowdy at midnight. I'm just saying that it's a bit crazy to send the kid to jail for it.

We have decided to lock people up for social deviancy these days. We tell ourselves that we're not running debtors' prisons, that this isn't Dickensian England, because we rarely lock people up for the simple fact of not having money. Instead, we lock them up for not paying court fines, or because poor people should know better than to be poor publicly, and because the cost of doing routine business in this country is the same whether you're rich or poor. And for the poor, that cost is way too high.

For example, I'd say my car is registered about three-quarters of the time, because sometimes the $50 it costs to renew the registration is more than I have to spare. At times, that's been more than a day's wages for me. And yes, I can go to jail for driving without proper registration. But if I'm too broke to renew, then I better get my ass to work, so I have to drive . . . and I'm guessing that you see where I'm going with this. In short: I'm fucked. Insurance I'm better about, because my life was upended by an uninsured driver. But I've been without it too—insurance companies aren't like the power company. They don't negotiate dates and payment plans. If you can't make your premium, you'll simply be uninsured until you can.

When I'm driving uninsured—because I have to get to work or buy toilet paper, the only two reasons the car moves in that situation—I take back roads and shop on the edge of town to avoid density and thereby lessen my likelihood of being in a fender bender. That'll get you sent to jail too, even if you're willing and able to pay the damages out-of-pocket.

The degree to which an accident or a traffic ticket could destroy my financial security—what little of it I have ever had—has made me a super-defensive driver. I don't take chances. I drive at precisely two miles over the limit, which is generally the sweet spot of not getting pulled over for speeding. If I drive more slowly than the limit, I worry that I'll be pulled over for curiosity's sake.

My policy of avoiding law enforcement is magnified when I'm behind the wheel of the car. It's my mission to appear as average as possible. Never stand out and never get hassled—unless we're in Arizona. (My husband is half Puerto Rican. He's pretty tan. We avoid Arizona like the plague. We've no interest in being asked to present his papers.)

So I go out of my way to give a wide berth to police and authority figures in general. There's no sense tempting fate. I'm sure most of them are lovely people, but I have no reason to trust anyone who has any sort of power over me. You can never be sure what they'll judge you for, and judgment has a nasty habit of turning into investigation.

For a long time, I have believed that most people think that poor people are criminals. Sound paranoid? Hear me out: Assuming you work in an office or white-collar environment, does your boss search your bag for stolen Post-its on your way out the door at night? No, I didn't think so. But I've had to surrender my bag at the end of my shift so security could search it and make sure I didn't swipe a box of pens or something. They did it to everyone, even each other. What kind of message does that send me? That I'm trusted? Or respected? Yeah, probably not. Instead, it tells me that my bosses think that if I have to work this crap job, then I'm definitely a thief. Or that they think I am so underpaid that I might steal out of necessity.

From there, it doesn't feel like much of a leap to conclude that rich people have written off an entire swath of America as trashy, careless, immoral, and irresponsible. And sure, some of us are. But some rich people are too. And if you had your bag searched every night, I guarantee you that you'd be sorely tempted to steal a few Post-it notes, just out of spite, if only to prove that you were smarter than they were.

This is a generalization, and I am once again going to take an opportunity to say that this is me talking; other people will feel differently about this. But overall, I think that most poor people have too many disasters in their own immediate future to worry about to be concerned about whatever natural or political disasters might be occurring way outside their circle.

I have a hippie friend. She's been known to dig through my trash for cans and drive them across the country to her favorite recycling center. I think she's crazy. It's not that I don't care about global warming or the environment; it's that there's only so far out of my way I'm willing to go. I don't really have the time or energy to worry about macro concerns.

Overconsumption is a concern for people who've made it to regular consumption.

I know people who are poor and environmentalists. It's not that poverty is guaranteed to make you callous, but being poor means that you are inherently unwasteful. Poor people just can't afford to buy a ton of extraneous shit and then throw it away barely used. So I don't really see a need to make the environment My Issue. I tend to eat food that is rejected by other people. (There are places you can buy nearly expired food for cheap.) I don't buy many things new at the store, because I can't generally afford it. I shop at thrift stores, where I can buy an almost-working bread machine for $2 and fix a wire. I combine all my errands into a single trip as a matter of course, because running to a store is generally more than a half-hour commitment and I want to save on gas.

I do not care about the whales. I'm unfussed about owls. I could give you a lot of reasons why I don't consider myself an environmentalist, but it mostly comes down to this: my issue is people, in the micro. Once we've hit the part where my own species is mostly taken care of, I'll start to worry about African rhinos. Until then, I'll just keep restraining myself from punching people when they look me in the face and argue that an ecosystem somewhere is more important than homelessness. It's not unimportant, and I'm glad someone is keeping an eye on those things, but right now it is nineteen degrees outside and there are some human beings that I am more concerned about saving just at the moment.

Poor people are busy keeping a roof over their own heads so that they, too, don't join the unhoused ranks. And that's about all that many of us have got time to be concerned about. Environmental concerns, campaign financing, civic engagement writ large—these are luxury worries for people with time and influence.

Do I wish that poor people were a little more politically engaged? Sure. I think that would help, and it sure as hell couldn't hurt. But I also get why people aren't beating down the doors of the polling places. For one, we can't keep track of whether we're supposed to bring a DNA sample or a urine sample this time to prove our identity and residency. It keeps changing. For another, the hours and polling locations in poorer neighborhoods keep getting cut for some reason. It is definitely not at all a conscious effort to repress the poor (read likely Democrat) vote. At all. Ever. (Dear GOP: You guys might want to police your people. They keep openly saying that your goal is to repress the vote of the poor.)

Additionally, at this point elections are mostly held for the benefit of people who devotedly follow politics. Everyone else kind of figures it's a done deal. Most districts are gerrymandered to the point of safety one way or another. Voting doesn't really enter into it, because no matter who stays home or heads out, more people in X party will vote.

Look, I'm not saying these are good reasons for not voting, but they're reasons that I can wrap my brain around.

What's harder for some people to understand is why poor people so often vote against our own self-interest. Even I have a difficult time with that one. Steinbeck said that we'd never be a socialist country because there were no poor Americans, only temporarily embarrassed millionaires. A lot of people really do think that way. I was raised by one. My dad talks like he's part of the top 5 percent. (Spoiler: He isn't.)

I have a Republican friend and every time we get into politics and the economy, he tells me that I simply don't understand the American dream. He says it doesn't make sense to punish the people you're trying to join. He is fairly certain that in the next decade or two, he will be worried about capital gains. He works at Walmart. He's nearing thirty. No degree, no real résumé, no particular ambition to do anything. Just a firm conviction that someday he'll have a fantastic high-powered career doing . . . something. He's not sure what, only that this is America and anyone can make it. While he's waiting, he'll be protecting his future interests at the ballot box.

But voting isn't always about money. My friend Rachel is a lovely woman. She's actually kind of a liberal on the money stuff but she's a strict Southern Baptist. She's also a firm GOP voter. She tells me that she's always been poor, she always will be poor, and it doesn't really matter to her whether or not the rich people get richer. At least, not in any way that's really going to affect her day-to-day. Systemically, sure, she'll give you that the economic policies advocated by her candidates are actually not great for her, but since she lives in a non-union area, it's much more important to her to have a candidate that's firm on the Second Amendment and abortion. Those things matter to her, in a real way, every day. She thinks about them, she knows people affected by them.

I tend to think that the economic policies aren't going to change much no matter how badly we want them to, but I'm sure that all my friends should be able to get married to whomever they wish, and I like the idea that I can get birth control without having to ask the blessing of the Republican leadership. Plus, I can't stomach supporting people who honestly think poor people are getting the long end of the stick. People that oblivious shouldn't be in charge of the free world, on principle.

So that's why I encourage everyone to vote for my guys. But I'm not about to judge a poor person who couldn't give a shit about any of it. That person hasn't been given a whole lot of proof that her vote will matter anyway; voting hasn't resulted in policy shifts toward a more equitable distribution of government services. Our schools are still worse, our roads less maintained, our police less friendly. And we simply don't give a fuck about quantitative easing or who might manage the prime index, because we do not have money and so those concerns are entirely irrelevant to us.

Poor people have gotten the message loud and clear: The powers that be are not concerned about us. Meanwhile, wealthier people get all exercised about a poor person dropping a cigarette butt on a city sidewalk, as if this is proof that poor people *just don't care.* Let's take that theory a step further. When powerful people stick a waste treatment plant in that same poor person's backyard, does that mean that rich people *just don't care?* I'm not even going to bother answering that one, because I think I already did.

Personally, I don't litter. It's not because I particularly feel any responsibility to the environment or anything. The reason I don't litter is that first, it's an insane ticket to pay if you don't have to, and second, it's one of the areas of my life where I get a bit fuck-you and refuse to live down to the expectations of rich people that I don't give a shit where I throw my trash. Besides, some poor asshole has to pick it up, and I try not to make people's jobs worse on principle.

It's always been interesting to me that we're expected to care about beautifying the roads or streets. I don't, really. Not until the places that I live get the same maintenance resources as the places where the mansions are.

If you wonder why I am angry sometimes, why I don't always feel a sense of human kinship with people wealthier than me, that's a pretty good example right there. They don't feel any toward me, and I'm under no obligation to be the bigger person. It seems like I'm expected to have the oblige, but I never get the noblesse. And yeah, no. I won't be doing that.

And now I'll finally say it: Some stereotypes exist for a reason. The bald front lawn and truck with no wheels, the pile of tires—these are all images that come to mind when you think of poor people. In fact, I am the proud owner of a tire pile, inherited from previous owners of my house. I can understand why you don't find that aesthetically pleasing. Hell, I don't find it aesthetically pleasing. But what I can't understand is why you'd judge the person who's too poor to pay the water bill to spray that dead lawn, or pay the mechanic's bill to fix that truck, or take the time off work to do something about those tires. (I saved up once and put in two rosebushes. They died because I was away at work too much to water them.)

Like most poor people, I have rented for most of my life, and some of my landlords have maintained my apartments so appallingly that I'm not exactly motivated to drop money I don't have on improving their property. When I finally did buy a house, I had enough to cover the mortgage but not to put money into something as frivolous as landscaping. My yard is pretty much dirt with some grass sprinkled here and there. I estimated the cost of putting grass in: It came to about a paycheck and a half, before we even considered the water bill.

While I'm on the topic, let me tell you about my house. You see, I have terrible, awful credit, mostly due to medical and student debt. There's no way in hell I'd find a mortgage. So when I was living in the trailer and got pregnant again, we needed space. I had my biological dad living with me, my husband, and one kid already, in a single-wide.

So we went looking for a place to rent, like you do. And what we found was nothing affordable. The only places we could have made rent on were either in student housing, which is not where you live if you're trying to get an infant to sleep, or were so beaten down that they would actually be unsafe, because you really shouldn't let babies play on surfaces with exposed nails.

So we asked my parents for help co-signing. What wound up happening is that they could refinance their own home for less than they could get a separate mortgage; they refinanced, paid cash from that for my house, and I pay *their* mortgage because it's sort of *my* mortgage. Understand that we are discussing a house that didn't even approach $100,000 here, so the monthly payments are reasonable. Better than any place we could find to rent. Those are the contortions that those of us who are lucky enough to have family help—

something that I have only recently had the luxury of—have to go through in order to participate in the economy.

Now back to the subject of maintaining that house. Yard care, which I hear is a relaxing pastime for many, is just another chore that I don't have time in the day for. There's no point paying for grass seed if you don't have a decent lawnmower and you never have an afternoon off to mow it.

So, okay, the ugly-lawn stereotype, I own that one and I don't really care what people think of me on that score. But the stereotype about bugs attaching themselves to poor people because we're dirty? That one pisses me off. I would like to take this opportunity to correct a common misimpression: You do not have to be a sloppy housekeeper to get bugs. That is some classist bullshit, right there. I've lived in places with roaches; they were there before me, and I'll place a public bet that the exact same roaches are still living there years after the fact. I tried everything. We stopped eating at home for two weeks so that there wouldn't be a single scrap of food in the place—they stayed. We put down poison— they stayed. We tried to smash them all—they wore down our resistance through sheer numbers. It was like being part of a single scout unit and finding an entire army just beyond the ridge; you've got no chance.

Roaches are nearly impossible to kill without repeated professional extermination treatments, and those ain't free. They live in walls and under woodwork; if there is a single crack in your apartment they can come in at will. Seriously, call your local exterminator and ask him if it is possible to stop a roach infestation with half a can of Raid in an apartment with cracked walls and a leaky sink. Start a timer from the end of your question and see how long it takes for him to stop laughing.

Bedbugs and lice like rich people as much as they like poor people. But if you're a poor person with either of those things, you will be judged. The only difference between a poor person with lice and a rich person with lice is that a rich person pays someone else to pick the nits out of her kid's hair. And if you're a poor person unlucky enough to get bedbugs, holy hell does your life suck. There isn't an effective pesticide for bedbugs—well, okay, there are two, but they're so toxic you can't spray them in your living space and then keep living there. Bedbugs can live for months without any sort of sustenance, and they also can live in ductwork and other places that you can't see when you're deciding whether or not to move into a place. You can't stop them once someone's introduced them into a building without some serious and expensive effort, and you can pick those things up on the bus, or at a gas station, or in a rented car, or at the airport, or generally anywhere in public.

Flies are inevitable when there are holes in your screens during the summer and your AC sucks or is nonexistent and you have to keep the windows open. They're easier to control through simple cleaning and some vigilant swatting than cockroaches, but they're a normal annoyance and a simple fact of life. That said, it's considered trashy to have flypaper up. You can't even win when you're clearly deploying effective containment measures.

Rodents living in holes in the walls of poor people's houses is such a common thing that mice were the entire supporting cast of Disney's *Cinderella*. Similar mice have starred in more than one children's movie since then. If you live in an older building, you'll get mice somewhere in it. I guess the upside is that you can pretend you're Cinderella, but I wouldn't hold out hope for any glass slippers coming your way.

Being poor: that's how you get ants. Having household pests isn't a result of a sloppy, irresponsible nature. It's a result of being broke. It's insulting and priggish to insist otherwise, especially if you're someone who actually pays someone to come to your home to clean for you.

Hey, I'm not blaming people for having those luxuries— I'd love to have them too. I've often thought that I need a wife. Or maybe a staff. I'm not really sure what would solve the problem, which is that there's always a time crunch. There just aren't enough minutes in the day for me to earn enough money and keep up on life's details and clean my house and maintain my yard and have a marriage and hang out with my kids. So my husband and I rank those things in order of importance by visibility: Are we the only people who see or have to live with this? Yes? Then who cares?

I really wish I were one of those naturally neat people. I'm not. I'm a natural slob. It takes some serious routine to get me to keep my house clean as a matter of course, but I'm normally too fucking tired when I get off work to clean, besides which I've been cleaning up after people all day. I'm rarely in the mood to carry on with that another couple hours when I only have eight hours off between shifts. My feet hurt, and my back is sore, and if I'd like both sleep and a shower, then wiping the grease off the oven isn't even on my list of priorities.

I always have way more stuff that I can neatly store. Anyone who has ever gone without can relate to this. Who knows when you might need something and can't afford to buy it? So I rarely throw anything away if I can store it and maybe use it in the future. Stained shirts might be useful rags for the one time in my life I get some furniture polish and motivation at the same time. My stash of ruined T-shirts made great diapers when my kids were babies. I've torn apart two broken coffeemakers to make one working one. You never throw anything away if one of the parts is working, because you might need that part eventually.

I tend to buy in bulk when I have the cash or if there's a really good sale. Right now there are probably ten bottles of laundry detergent in my closet, because I found it so cheap.

I go to discounters and wait until the snacks actually expire, at which point they're ten cents or a quarter for a whole bag of chips. Granted, the only reason they sit around that long is that they're off-brand and actually kind of gross (I have seen chips that were supposed to taste like BBQ ranch and cheddar and sour cream all at once, which I think we can all agree is just the worst thing humans have invented), but you can give them to the kids and they'll never notice. Or you can have a couple beers and you won't really care either.

I guess some people would call all this kind of shameless. And that's what this whole discussion about civics, and citizenship, and personal responsibility comes down to: self-respect, or a perceived lack thereof. Most privileged people have enough compassion to feel badly for people who don't have money. But unfortunately, a not-insignificant percentage of advantaged people have a hard time understanding that shame is a luxury item, because there is a point at which things are so bad that you lose all sense of shame.

Shameless is admitting that you're poor and asking for money. It's being brazen. It's having sex in public because you've got nowhere else to go. It's openly selling drugs when that's what you do for a living. I'm not going to try to defend hard-core drug dealers. They're indefensible—unless they are on TV, in which case we are fascinated by them. But most "drug dealers," in fact, are people who essentially share weed with their friends at cost. They're not looking to morally flatten their neighborhoods; they just don't see anything wrong with people getting a little high instead of a little drunk. And pushing dime bags is enough to pay a bill or two, keep your phone or gas on, and keep your car moving.

That's desperation. And I'll tell you something else shamelessness can lead you to: selling your food stamps. Is that illegal? Yup. Is it understandable? Yup. If you are willing to live on nothing but ramen, you'll have at least $20 left over on your food stamp card. You can then, completely hypothetically and I have never done this, engage in a transaction with a neighbor. They get food, and in return you get $10 for your gas tank. Your neighbor will do you this favor so that you will take them in the car you now have gas for to cash their paycheck, which they need to do to replace the $10 they just gave you for gas anyway. That's what we mean by hustling; you have to figure out who's good for what at any given time so that you can find rides and babysitters and small loans. You also need everyone to know what you can be counted on for, because that is your bartering token.

Is that shameless? Maybe. Shameless is something that happens when you have been pushed beyond shame, when you have nothing left to lose. If you will shortly be homeless, what have you got to lose by begging in the street? Maybe you will avert the disaster. If not, you've simply gotten a head start on your new station in life.

"Trashy" is a word that has two meanings. It can mean classless, hitting *Maury* levels of public airing of personal behavior. Or it can mean unkempt, which is largely a function of how much time and money you have to spend on maintaining your house and person.

Trashy, the insult, means that you embody the poor-white-person stereotypes. Trashy is what you call people who have brought their eighteen-month-old to the restaurant and are letting him gleefully tear paper napkins and tortillas apart and scatter the pieces on the floor around him like so much confetti. Trashy is talking loudly on your phone in the bathroom. Trashy is using your outside voice to have personal conversations in public areas that are decidedly inside.

My husband, who's from the West Virginia part of Ohio, says that in the sticks where he's from, you can always tell a trashy person because their chickens are out. If you build a chicken coop out of reclaimed fencing and duct tape, you're not necessarily trashy. But you'd better damn well keep your chickens in that coop and off the road.

Okay, so we've established this: Poverty isn't pretty. We can't afford to dress nicely. Our yards are a mess. We don't really care about your political pet projects. But do you know what we really do care about? Each other. And I'm going to make a big leap here that I am very comfortable with: Poor people are, as a rule, a bit more generous. We understand what it might be like to have to beg even if we have never done it ourselves. In fact, there's data to back me up. The latest research shows that people of low socioeconomic status are more likely to be altruistic than their higher-class counterparts. In 2011, the bottom 20 percent of earners gave a higher percentage of their wealth away than the top 20 percent.

I'll put it to you this way: If good citizenship consists of a well-ordered life, then we poor people make terrible citizens. But if it means being willing to help out your fellow human beings, I'd say we're right out in front waving a flag and waiting for everyone else to get on the bandwagon.

10

An Open Letter to Rich People

Dear Rich People,

I know that nobody understands you. I want to help. I have, for all my faults, always been rather compassionate to people who are in real pain.

I know that you understand what I mean when I say that sometimes I feel so unappreciated that I just can't be bothered to care. See? There. I feel your pain.

So to make it easier, I have some observations, some advice. Because if there's anything a poor person knows about, it's how to survive in this fucked-up world.

And seriously? You people are doing it wrong.

1. WORK

What is it with you people and your meetings? I've been allowed to sit in on a few of them recently. I don't know how you stand them. Suddenly, the insane rules you people make us live with seem inevitable. See, until I started sitting in on the meetings, I couldn't see a single reason for programs that had contradictory rules or relief programs that were practically inhumane in their lack of realism. Now I realize it's because every meeting results in nobody having a clue what they've actually done. They've been devoting only 10 percent of their brains to the meeting itself, the remainder being occupied with fantasies of mayhem and whatever song they last heard. Here are my observations from one such meeting:

- I'd have been fired from all my regular jobs if I made my bosses repeat themselves this much.
- WE HAVE BEEN OVER THIS SO MANY TIMES ALREADY!
- If time is money, how does this world function?
- Holy balls, the flattery.
- So many people not paying attention right now.
- Why are they reading the handout to us? I think everyone here can read.

- Is it possible that there is actually no point to this meeting?

I'm not kidding, rich people. You can email me for a copy of the notes.

I've just been sitting through meetings wondering when the work would get done. What I have discovered is this: In every one of them, someone opens by talking about how we want to be respectful of everyone's time and right to speak, along with a plea to keep comments short. Then everyone sort of tunes out while the agenda is being read. Some talking is done by whoever is running things, mostly follow-up from the last meeting.

Then the fun begins. Someone will rise, bring up a good point. Someone else will clarify. A third will ask a relevant question. And then—and here's the part that gets me every time—someone will ask a question that makes it perfectly clear that they weren't paying the slightest bit of attention during the last ten minutes or so. *And nobody calls them out for it.* As long as the question or observation is worded just a little differently, it counts as a new contribution. What the fuck, rich people? Time is money, unless that time is being spent repeating things that have been established already?

Worse are the endless reassurances. "I don't want you to think I'm opposed, because it's a fantastic idea you had to buy ten crocodiles and set them loose in a school as a publicity stunt, but I just don't think it'll work for us." Why on earth do you people not just tell each other when your ideas suck? Why the self-esteem dance? You guys, you're allowed to have bad ideas and irrelevant points. It does not make you a terrible human being. Maybe you should just accept that and then you don't have to cover any criticism, even the most gentle, in five minutes of apology. Maybe we could borrow some of your apology time for our workdays, and then both of our problems would be solved.

By the end of the meeting, which inevitably has run over by at least twenty minutes, nobody is entirely sure what's been accomplished, but everyone feels like their concerns were heard. I have come to the conclusion that business meetings are like group therapy for the wealthy. Everyone sits around looking at each other and waiting for it to be their turn to speak so that they can zone out for the remainder of the time they aren't allowed to leave the room.

The meetings are what made me realize that you guys slack off at work too. It's just that you don't call it slacking off (and that you all have office doors to close so no one can see you playing solitaire or shopping online).

So, rich people, now that we've established that your work ethic and approach to your job are not exactly unassailable, how about you get off your high horse about how we poor people do our jobs? Also:

- Please stop equating our jobs. I am not saying that you put in no effort, that you're not tired or overburdened or anything. I just think that we should delineate between the jobs where you can pee at will and the ones where you can't.

- For the love of God, please stop telling us that outrageous salaries are justified because some people are just worth that much. You guys can totally pretend that anyone can possibly justify earning thousands of dollars every minute. Just stop demanding that we pretend with you, that's all. You guys are supergood at excluding us from conversations. Maybe make that one of them. Just let me know when you start gossiping and I'll rejoin the conversation. I bet someone got laid.

- Maybe you could hire us? I hear rich people complaining about being overworked. I hear poor people complaining about being unemployed. I feel like there's a solution here. You know we work cheap, right? You could totally pay me $10 that one time to run your errands for you or write that standard report that's a pain because it's such rote work. *We are highly trained in rote work.*

2. CIVICS

This is a big one for me. See, civics is the study of citizenry, its burdens and responsibilities and privileges. It's more than whether or not you, as a class, vote frequently. It's about whether or not you'd want to live in the nation you've created; if you were born tomorrow into the lower classes, would you be quite so sure that America is the land of opportunity? (See what I did there? That's *philosophy*. I am trying to speak in your language here, rich people. Because I care deeply about how your day is going today.)

Do I think rich people are highly hypocritical in this area. Um, yeah. Shall I delineate further?

- If you're the makers, *what do you make?* I make food and fill boxes and exchange goods for money. Please find a different word, rich people, besides *makers*. Maybe you could try "magicians," because you can create money where there was none before. And then please teach me how to do that too.

- I know it's a pipe dream, but maybe you guys can just admit that we all get shit (see entitlements, roads, tax credits, crop subsidies, fire departments) from the government and move on with your lives?

- It's relatively easy to keep a neighborhood looking nice if the local government actually maintains the roads and medians and signs. If they are too busy making sure that the already-nice sections of town stay that way, they do not have time to come improve the not-nice parts. This is why we laugh when you wonder why we live in run-down areas. It's because when public service cuts happen, they never happen in the bougie neighborhoods. You should know that, given that it's being reported in all your media outlets.

- Your dogs do not belong in restaurants even if they are supercute. I swear to God, the number of tiny dogs I've seen in inappropriate places is at least ten times higher than the number of times I've gotten laid in my life. And, newsflash: Only service animals are allowed in restaurants. That's actually a public health concern. I don't get why you're allowed to decide you're completely above the law simply because you found a purse to fit your dog into.

3. ATTITUDE

So, okay, sometimes I have a shitty attitude. I'll give you that. But at least I'm not often entitled. People in the upper classes are so used to having everything done for them that they get sort of irrational and start to feel like you're person-ally attacking them for not being honestly pleased to see them. It's a bit off-putting, to say the least, to have someone sweep in like that.

- If you think poor people are entitled, try denying a rich person with an attitude some service they think they've earned. It's like grief—there are phases. Anger and denial are first. Then comes "do you understand how fucked you are if I don't get the thing I want?" Followed by "I demand to see your manager" and "I've never been treated so poorly in my life." The final stage is bargaining, where they try to give you extra money because all of life is like valet service to them, and an extra five bucks can change the world.

- If that doesn't convince you, try wearing stained or unintentionally torn (professionally torn is fine and thus useless for these purposes) clothes and sitting on a stoop somewhere. Note how many rude comments or nasty glares you get from well-dressed people. Being rich is like being white, you guys. It's not that sometimes your life doesn't suck even if you're white. It's that you're not allowed to complain about the two times being white is unhandy, because all of your alternatives are much unhandier. Your other options are any race or ethnicity but white, all of whom face normal human shitty existence *and* racism of the entrenched or overt variety. It's the same thing being rich. I'm not saying that sometimes you don't get the short end of the stick. All I'm saying is that you look ridiculous whining about how you just can't make ends meet on $200,000 because you have to spend so much money to survive. You come off as petulant and incapable of managing the slightest taste of reality when the raising of the capital gains tax back to what you paid under Clinton is cast as a brimstone-filled apocalypse. Sometimes you just have to bite your tongue and keep your mouths shut to avoid looking like assholes.

• Barack Obama caused a flap because he told rich people that they weren't the sole factors in their own success. You are not allowed to do that, because wealthy people are far too precious to face the idea that they didn't do it all themselves, or spring out of the womb, fully formed, as hotshot entrepreneurs or whatever they want us to see them as. I cannot fathom actually thinking that the entire world must collaborate to hide reality from me, and on top of that hubris, being upset when someone dares to speak a distasteful truth. You guys have got to get tougher than that.

4. HEALTH

I have no idea what a wealthy person's health care experience is typically like. I've never had that. But I do know that some of the things I see more comfortable folks doing look pretty stupid, and I tend to trust the people with the advanced degrees and years of experience when it comes to how things like cars or bodies work. At least I do if what they want me to do is reasonable and attainable. I only ignore the stuff that's out of reach. You guys, though—seriously, why even bother going to the doctor at all if you think you know everything?

- I am so sorry, rich people. It has to suck to have enough money to stay healthy, because then you don't have an excuse for aging. You have to *maintain*.

- On the other hand, some of the shit you people will pay for blows my mind. Like lotion with actual pearls ground up in it. Actual. Pearls. I stopped at a mall cart to ask about the stuff. It's obscenely expensive. I think that's because you're literally smearing semiprecious materials all over your face.

- You seriously need to control yourselves with the surgical anti-aging. You're starting to look . . . weird. At least we in the lower classes rarely have to live with botched plastic surgery. Very few poor women have someone over-collagenate their lips or paralyze their foreheads. Poverty has its privileges, and one of them is not having to worry about where the line between beauty standard and malpractice lawsuit is.

- We use home remedies because they are cheap, not because they are superior to all of Western medicine. If you can afford a real doctor and you prefer an herbalist, you have lost all sense of reason.

- You guys pay people actual cash money for the privilege of becoming physically exhausted. Has it occurred to you all that you could probably run, for free, on the streets—that you do not actually need to pay money to a gym for the privilege of running on a treadmill? I said that to a wealthy woman once, and she told me that she preferred to work out in air-conditioning. It is possible that I am fundamentally misunderstanding something here, but I thought that sweating was a *good* thing when you're trying to lose weight?

- Concierge doctors. I am totally cool with people having on-call physicians. But I do think it makes you look like assholes to have your own special VIP offices. Doctors do that, you know; they have a regular office and waiting room for regular patients, and a swanky spa setup for the boutique patients. *It is the same doctor.* You are not getting the benefit of more expertise, he's just kissing your ass more in a slightly more refined setting. If you make the (valid) argument that you get more time, as well, I will just say this: Can you please hire special nurses to listen to your worries about this discolored spot you just discovered on your arm? There are already not enough doctors to go around.

I promise you, a talented nurse is as good as a doctor in most cases.

5. COPING

I am certain that you have stress, rich people. Nobody's life is perfect. I am equally certain that your stress and my stress are only similar in that they are called the same thing. I take plenty of shit for my habits and vices; what I simply cannot stand by and allow to happen is for you to escape with no notice. I am sorry, guys, but I'm forcing you out of the human closet.

- You know who smokes? Rich people and poor people. You know what that means? *Rich people smoke too.* I'm not kidding, I've seen them at it. I even loaned my lighter to a couple of them, just so I could touch their hands and verify that they weren't holograms or something. With as much shit as I've taken in my life for having such a nasty, wasteful, stupid habit, I'd assumed that wealthy people would be much too good for something so déclassé. But nope, they're on the streets getting

cancer with the rest of us. I think I'm done hearing
about why poor people smoke. I don't know, why do
rich people smoke? I'm willing to bet that our ratio-
nales are pretty fucking similar.

- You guys look pretty ridiculous talking about our
  drug and alcohol use while swanky rehab centers
  are doing a thriving business. It might behoove you
  to just admit that addiction is terrible and can hit
  anyone; otherwise we're probably going to have to
  start pointing out your raging prescription drug
  abuse problem. And you wouldn't want that; as it
  turns out, it's kind of embarrassing when people
  accuse you of copious drug use.

6. SEX

Tell me, how many of you were virgins when you got married? So, our sex lives are up for discussion how again? For
all the concern about underprivileged people fucking with
reckless abandon, you guys sure don't seem to hold yourselves to a higher standard.

- I know this argument has been made everywhere. But it's valuable. So here it is: You cannot cut access to birth control and then act surprised when people get pregnant. I am fairly certain that few wealthy people walk around with that infamous cheap aspirin between their knees. Poor people are allowed to fuck sometimes too! And we do! Because we're human! *Just like you!*

- You really need to start using condoms or something. Your STD rates are pretty much the same as ours. It's hard to listen to you guys on public health issues when you're getting the clap as often as we are.

- I know that we, the lower classes, tend to speak more frankly and openly than you guys do, as we lack a proper sense of rich-person propriety. So it is very possible that you do not know much about BDSM, and that would explain the success of the *Fifty Shades* franchise. But I worry about you without any plainspoken poor people to tell you what's what, so please listen closely: *You need a safe word.* Do not, rich people, attempt bondage on your own. Please find a high-end sex club for your wanton romps.

7. PARENTING

I disapprove of about as many of the upper class's child-rearing habits as they do of mine. Rich and poor are different, you see, and as such, we value different things. I have trouble with the way you're raising your kids. They're not all special precious unicorns, destined to cure cancer. And if you tell them that they are, they feel entitled to act as though it were true.

You can stop this cycle, rich people. Just teach your kids that they're human like everyone else. Maybe a special snowflake, but one that will still get in trouble if they misbehave on the playground. I have faith in your ability to heal the next generation. I am counting on you, rich people. Don't let me down.

- One word: nannies. You cannot call anyone out on their parenting skills if they're doing as much of the parenting as you are—or more of it. It's great that you hired someone with advanced degrees and multiple languages to sing Junior to sleep—more power to you. But I don't see the difference between hiring a nanny or two so you can attend to the rest of life and dropping your kid with a sitter for the same reason. *It's the same thing.*

- And the kids' accessories! I know I already talked a bit about this, but how much shit do you actually think an average toddler really needs? I have a weakness for bouncy balls and coloring books, and my kids get a ton of those. You know what they don't have? Anything that says Giorgio Armani on it. Because it's fucking silly to put designer anything on a kid.

- We feel bad for your kids, rich people. Your kids aren't allowed to be kids. Your kids have tutors by the time they're three and start taking standardized tests in preschool. Your kids have parents who seriously think it's a bad idea to just let them play with sticks and rocks, who think that's actually objectively bad parenting. Loosen up a bit. They'll survive it, and so will you.

- I promise you, you don't need a titanium stroller. You just don't. I thought I had the Range Rover of strollers when I got a normal-size one instead of the folding metal-pipe travel kind. But then I recently spent some time in upscale neighborhoods, and I realized that I had been wrong. I'd had the midsize stroller; the super-big ones come with not just a place for your kid but a place for your groceries and an attached activity center for Junior and wheels with extra shocks. I had the perverse impulse to ask a woman how much hers had run, and she told me. After that, I am assuming that this stroller also picks up the dry cleaning and will murmur sweet nothings into your ear on command. I've bought cars for less than half what an expensive stroller runs.

- Science disapproves of your antibacterial-spray fetish. Kids need to develop immunities, you see, which they do partially from coming into contact with germs. Not to mention, you're actually creating superbugs, bacteria that are resistant to our killing methods. I'm gonna be pissed if I get some superflu because you were afraid Johnny might catch a cold, that's all I'm saying.

- I am seriously disappointed in you for bringing back measles with the anti-vaccination kick. And whooping cough. Get on that, rich people. You need to self-police. Seriously, guys, I'm a mother. I understand wanting to protect your children. All I'm saying is that maybe you could protect the kids from the mumps. Maybe we can start there.

8. PRACTICALITIES

I hope that at this point you are feeling like maybe you hadn't thought this whole stratification thing through all the way. You guys don't really ever talk to us and have no idea what our daily lives are like. But we watch and notice what you do when you are politely ignoring us. And I have some parting words of wisdom: When you think of your stacks of cash, remember that they are gifts, simple things put into your lives to make them easier. You get to have those things. Fucking enjoy them or pass them to the left, man.

- You guys completely take the little things for granted. If you are sleepy while you are driving, you just pull over and find a hotel. If your car breaks down, you call a shop. If you are sick, you go to a doctor. If you break a heel, you get a new pair of shoes. Appreciate that, assholes.

- Money doesn't buy happiness. It buys ease. You can make your life pleasant and enjoyable, get yourself a decent mattress and thus a decent night's sleep. Will it make you happy? Not a chance. But it doesn't hurt.

- If you guys are so good with money, then what do financial planners do? Put another way, maybe you're good with money because you're paying someone to sort out the details?

- Warranties are awesome. They only come on things you buy new. This is why all our shit is broken and yours isn't; you get a grace period after you buy something in which you can be pretty sure you won't have to buy it again, because if it breaks it's under warranty.

- As long as you keep holding me accountable for not making it when I was well under the national median income, I'll hear no whining about how difficult it is to find good help. (Pro tip on the help, rich people: Treat us fairly, pay us decently, and make it clear that you give half a fuck whether we live or die. We'll kill ourselves for you.)

And there you have it, rich people. I hope it helps.

Afterword

You've got a thousand more questions than you did when you started the book, don't you? When did we start reliving the Gilded Age? What do you mean they can fire you for no reason? Why bother trying at all if poor people are so fucked from the start?

Well, because we don't have an option. Millions of people every day aren't feeling particularly hopeful that today will be the day it all turns around—but we still look for a job that's marginally better than what we've got. Just in case. When all of your options are as bad as the next, you take your pick and, yes, you hope for the best. Sometimes those decisions turn out to be less than great. Occasionally that's on me. I'm only human, after all, and I make mistakes. But as often as not, the poor outcome was destined from the start. You can't choose between a terrible option and a dreadful option and come out of it whistling a happy tune. You can try to dismiss my depiction of poverty as being representative of just one person's experience, but I am not an aberration. Millions of people have had to shake their asses for Walmart.

Hopefully that last paragraph answered some of your questions. I'm sorry that I don't know the answers to all of them. But I know exactly how you can find out: Ask someone.

There are poor and working-class people everywhere, guys. You can just have a conversation with one, like a real human being. Give it a try. You'll like it. We're entertaining. We have to be; we're stuck entertaining each other because cable is ridiculously expensive.

I don't claim to be an expert. I don't know what we do to solve the problems of stratification. What I do know is that we can and have to do better than this. We're so far behind the curve on these issues that we're having a public fight about whether or not the poor are too comfortable. (Hi, Paul Ryan!) It's not fucking pleasant to be poor. It's not a free ride, a gentle swing in the hammock. It's what's left when you've lost everything, when you're fighting to survive as opposed to fighting to get ahead.

If you feel that something must be done before the villagers find their pitchforks, here is what you can do: Stop being a dick to service workers whenever possible. Start filling out those stupid surveys when someone's done their job well, because they really do make us get a quota of them. Stop pretending you're doing us a favor or performing some high moral duty by refusing to tip. And start admitting that you need us as much as we need you.

And the next time you feel as though you're shouldering more than your fair share of society's burdens, ask yourself: How badly do I have to pee right now, and do I need permission?

Acknowledgments

Mollie Glick, at Foundry, decided to be my agent and I wish her nothing but bestsellers in the future. I additionally hope that the next person she decides to make into an author has more idea what she is doing than I did. Amy Einhorn has a wicked sense of humor and is an amazing editor, and any praise you care to name should go in her direction. Thankfully, she put me in touch with Peternelle van Arsdale, who not only knows where to find good food but is adept at pulling half-formed thoughts from your brain and turning them into sense. Rodney Staton deserves thanks for patient questioning and teaching while I tried to get my brain in order.

I'd also like to thank:

Sara Benincasa, for keeping me posted and sending me into the best sales pitch in history; Alexis Welby, for being incredibly patient with me in general and also for an insane amount of stress tolerance; Kirsten Neuhaus, for coordinating details through time zones and making it work somehow; and all the people at Foundry who worked on my stuff that I don't even know about. Emily Brown and Katie Grinch, for taking my calls even when I had that tone and emailing me things endlessly when I lost the last thing in my inbox. And the people at Penguin: Ivan Held and Kate Stark, Andrea Ho and Lisa Amoroso, Linda Rosenberg, Meredith Dros, and Maureen Klier, as well as all the people I don't know to name, because all of you spent time making this thing come together. I won't pretend to have a clue how, but I really appreciate it. Finally, Liz Stein, who picked up the baton and ran with it like a pro.

Barbara Ehrenreich, who spoke for me without knowing it years ago, and whose encouragement came at just the right time.

John Oliver and Andy Zaltzman, for Hotties from History.

To everyone I have met along the way: You are all amazing in some way. I'm sorry for the times I have not been my best self, and grateful for the times you have been yours. Mostly, I am probably glad to have met and hung out with you. Four of you can seriously go fuck yourselves.

To my parents: Thank you for making me read. That getting-me-to-adulthood-alive thing was pretty hairy. I mean, looking back, I'd have put a leash on me too. Sorry about the tattoos. I'm still not ruling out another one. And to my children: I damn well waited until I was eighteen. You'll rule everything out until I'm not legally responsible for your stupidity. I love you, but sadly for you, I love you too much to let you be stuck at seventeen forever. That would be hell.

Nancy Stalnaker, Crystal Corrigan, and Jacob Leonard, for things they know about as well as general awesomeness: You're all ninjas. Ryan Clayton: The inscription was right. I can't say it better than that. Brianne Grebil: You renewed some much-needed faith in humanity. Thank you for random awesomeness.

Tom: I don't even think there are words. Thank you for giving me the time I needed to write in, keeping the kids from destroying my work, and insisting on silly cartoons when I needed them. You're the best, and the Independents will be on my playlist until I die.

Chritter, Slay Belle, and all the other mods in the places I was hanging out last fall: You're the best. Internet people in general: I have learned more about the world from interacting with you in the last few years than I had in my entire life. If ever I conduct myself correctly and with grace, it's because I'm thinking of the stuff you all had the patience to teach me. And if ever I land a hell of a one-liner, it's because I learned from the best.

Finally, to everyone who has read this and known exactly what I was talking about: You have earned more than you think you have. It is your right to demand it, and you do not need to ask for favors. I hope that you get a decent gig and get on top of things soon. You work for your paycheck, but you have earned dignity and respect. That is yours, and fuck anyone who tries to tell you otherwise.